WHY and WHEN

By MARY ELTING and FRANKLIN FOLSOM

Illustrated by W. K. PLUMMER

ODHAMS BOOKS

LONDON · NEW YORK · SYDNEY · TORONTO

Foreword

ALL AROUND the world, people tell stories about the ancient quarrel between dogs and cats. In Romania, the story is told this way:

Long ago, Adam had a dog and a cat. The two animals made an agreement: The dog was to guard the outside of Adam's house and the cat, the inside. They wrote the agreement on a piece of paper, and the cat put it away in the house for safekeeping.

After that, they lived quite peacefully until one day the devil came by. Now, if there was one thing the devil could not stand, it was friendly cooperation. So he got the dog to thinking that the agreement was unfair because it kept him outdoors in all kinds of weather. Finally, the dog went to the cat and complained.

"An agreement is an agreement," said the cat.

"Let me see what we wrote down," said the dog.

The cat went to get the agreement, but found that mice had eaten it. This made the cat angry, and she started to chase mice.

When she didn't bring the agreement, the dog, too, became angry. He started to chase her, and dogs have been chasing cats ever since.

If you ask an archeologist when it was that dogs started to chase cats, he may tell you that it has been going on for at least four thousand years. It seems that scientists dug into an ancient buried city in India and found a curious brick that is four thousand years old. When this brick was still soft and wet — before it was baked — two animals left their pawprints on it. The paws belonged to a dog and a cat, and the prints show clearly that the cat was running away from the dog.

6

Ask a biologist when dogs started chasing cats, and he may point out that dogs have a habit of chasing many things, particularly things that move. A greyhound at a racetrack even runs after a mechanical gadget that looks like a rabbit. Dogs are born with this chasing habit, and it once was important. They got their food by running and catching other animals.

We have no real way of telling when all this began. So we have no precise answer to the question, "When did dogs start chasing cats?"

There are many such questions that can't be answered exactly, although it is fun to try. This book will skip most of the unanswerable kind. Instead, it will try to tell when or why or how or where things really happened long ago — and who or what made them happen. Many of these questions are very small windows to the past, and it may surprise you to discover that a small window can often give a very big view.

Mary Elting and Franklin Folsom

CONTENTS

WHEN DID IT HAPPEN?

ONE DAY several years ago, people all around the world saw what seemed to be a new star in the sky. It was indeed something new — a huge, silvery balloon that caught and reflected light from the sun. An American rocket had just put it into orbit around the earth. The balloon was a satellite named *Echo II* which space scientists had built for experiments with radio broadcasting. Both the United States and the Soviet Union could use it. For the first time in history, those two countries were going to cooperate in a space project.

According to the calendars of both countries, *Echo II* was launched on the 25th day of the month of January, A.D. 1964. This means 1,964 years after the birth of Jesus. The letters *A.D.* are an abbreviation of *Anno Domini,* Latin words meaning "in the year of our Lord."

Other countries have different ways of telling when things happen. The captions with the pictures give some of them. Not one of these ways is perfect, but the Christian or Western calendar is the one that has spread to most parts of the modern world. Why? Because Western Europeans took it with them when they began to carry their business dealings and scientific knowledge around the world about five hundred years ago.

In Japan, the date for the launching of *Echo II* is the 25th day of the beginning month of the 39th year of *Showa*. *Showa* is the Japanese name for the whole reign of Emperor Hirohito. The reign of each emperor has its own name.

According to the calendar used by religious Jews, *Echo II* went into orbit on 11 *Shebat, 5724*. This was 5,724 years after the date on which Orthodox Jews believe the world was created.

Moslems say *Echo II* was launched on the 10th of *Ramadan,* A.H. 1383. The letters "A.H." stand for "in the year of the *Hegira*." The *Hegira* was the journey made by Mohammed, the founder of the Moslem's religion, after his enemies forced him to flee from the city of Mecca in Arabia.

According to one kind of traditional Chinese calendar used on the island of Taiwan, *Echo II* was launched on the 25th day of the first month of the 53rd year of the Chinese Republic. Another kind of Chinese calendar is based on the appearance and disappearance of the moon. It would give this same date as the 11th day of the 18th month of the 40th year of the 77th 60-year cycle of the moon. The Western calendar also is used on Taiwan.

The People's Republic of China on the mainland of Asia is not Christian, but it uses the Western calendar, which got its present form from Pope Gregory of the Roman Catholic Church.

Although the date is not given in the Bible, many Christian scholars say Jesus was born in the year A.D. 1. Others, using clues in the New Testament, put the date of his birth between 20 and 15 B.C. The letters are an abbreviation for "before Christ." Still other scholars give various dates — between 9 and 6 B.C. or as late as A.D. 6. Even if everybody finally agreed that the date was *not* A.D. 1, we would probably keep the present calendar for convenience.

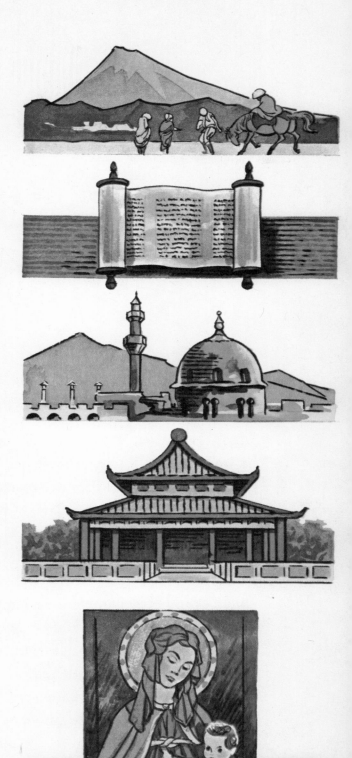

WHY DOES TRAFFIC GO TO THE RIGHT IN SOME COUNTRIES BUT TO THE LEFT IN OTHERS?

MOST PEOPLE in every part of the world are born right-handed. So far as we know, they always have been. We can be quite sure of this because scientists have found many ancient stone tools with edges worn down in a way that shows use by right-handed people. They have found fewer left-handed tools. Since men held their spears and daggers in the right hand, they carried their shields in the left. Whenever armed travellers met on a trail, each one preferred to have the stranger on his left where his shield would protect him, and so he walked on the right side of the pathway.

Roman soldiers, who used shields, were trained to keep to the right of the road, and Roman roads spread over much of Europe. This military custom was one important reason why ordinary people got into the habit of passing to the right. There were other reasons, too. Horse-drawn wagons came into use in Europe about A.D. 1000, and the teams were led, not driven. To control a team, most men held the head of the lead horse with a strong right hand and arm. This meant that all of the horses in the team walked on the driver's right. If the road was good, he wanted to stay on it and let the team go off into the mud. Of course, when two drivers met and passed, their wagons also kept to the right.

12

After drivers began to ride instead of walk, they followed the same traffic pattern. A man sat on the left rear horse in his team. This made it easy for him to reach every horse with a whip held in his right hand. Later, when wagons had seats, drivers simply moved back onto the left side of the seat. From this position, it was easier to guide the horses if traffic kept to the right.

After firearms came into use in the 1400's, a rider on horseback had a new reason for following the old custom: He carried his musket in the crook of his left arm. If he travelled on the right side of the road, the weapon was always pointed toward any stranger he met.

In the very beginning, Englishmen and other Europeans had the same reasons for keeping to the right. But about nine hundred years ago, things changed. Knights became more important in England than they were in most other countries, and they made a sport of fighting on horseback. They called it jousting. Two knights, clad in armour, would charge at each other. They carried spears or swords and each tried to knock the other off his horse. In order to play this game — or to have a serious fight on horseback — a knight had to have his opponent on his right. This meant passing to the *left*. Knights became used to riding on the left side of the road, and other English riders imitated them.

Later, Englishmen no longer jousted or wore armour, but they still carried swords, and they continued the old traffic custom when they met strangers on trails or bridges. Since they did not have shields, it was safer to keep any other swordsman on the right.

This aristocratic custom was adopted by the lower classes in England. Traffic to the left gradually became fixed, and the custom spread to almost all the places within the British Empire or where Englishmen had special influence.

However, when English colonists first settled in North America, they had no horses, so there was no reason to keep English traffic habits. At the same time, on the woodland trails, they carried their muskets in the crook of the left arm and walked to the right for safety. When horses arrived, riders carried guns, not swords, so the right-hand traffic continued. Wagoners and coachdrivers followed the pattern of the riders.

WHEN WERE THE FIRST TRAFFIC LAWS MADE?

FOR THOUSANDS of years, there were customs but no laws about keeping to the right or keeping to the left on roads. In many places, there was not much need for laws. Most country roads in England, for example, used to be very broad. There was always room enough for wagons or carts to pass each other, and there were no traffic jams. But in 1555, all this began to change. In that year, a law forced ordinary men to keep roads repaired without pay. People naturally wanted to do as little of this work as possible, so they made the roads narrow. And as soon as roads became narrow, traffic problems began. Some men proposed that there should be laws requiring all traffic to go to the right, as in the old Roman tradition. Others favoured the left-hand traffic that had started with English knights and that had continued with aristocratic riders on horseback. The custom of the riders won .

In 1756, the English Parliament passed an act that required carriages on London Bridge to keep to the left. Parliament made left-hand traffic

14

the general rule for all of Britain in 1835. Rules made for horse-drawn wagons were continued when automobiles came along, and they spread to many countries that were governed or greatly influenced by Britain.

In France, the first traffic law was made by King Louis XIV in the seventeenth century. At that time, some of the streets of Paris were too narrow for two carriages to pass each other, so Louis decreed that the one belonging to the less important man would have to back up. This caused arguments. Men would stand in the street reciting their family history, each claiming to be the more aristocratic. Strangers often stepped in to settle the quarrels.

One of the first traffic laws in North America, passed in 1787, stated that carriages, wagons or sleighs going north had to back up or turn out upon meeting a vehicle going south.

Sweden long followed the left-hand custom, but the Swedish Government finally decided that after September 3, 1967, all cars must travel on the right side of the road.

WHY DID THE INDIANS SELL MANHATTAN FOR $24?

WHEN SETTLERS from Holland came to the New World, they wanted to build a town on the island called Manhattan at the mouth of the Hudson River, so they approached a group of Indians on the island and paid them 60 guilders, about $24. For a long time afterward, people said that foolish Indians had been tricked by clever Europeans into giving up valuable property. The fact is that the Indians did not have the same idea about land that the Dutch had. To the white men, land represented property and wealth. It was something that could be bought and sold. To the Indians, land was just there — like the ocean or the air. You could have the right to use it, but how could you own it?

In exchange for the gift the Dutchmen gave, the Indians were happy to let these strangers join them in using the wooded island. Plainly, what the Indians "sold" and what the Dutch bought were two very different things. In addition, it seems quite possible that the Indians who accepted the money did not even live there! They may have been just passing by.

Such misunderstandings happened time and again as Europeans moved into America. They assumed that Indians would think about land as they did. So arguments arose between the two different kinds of people who never understood each other. The Europeans finally won, because they outnumbered the Indians and had better weapons.

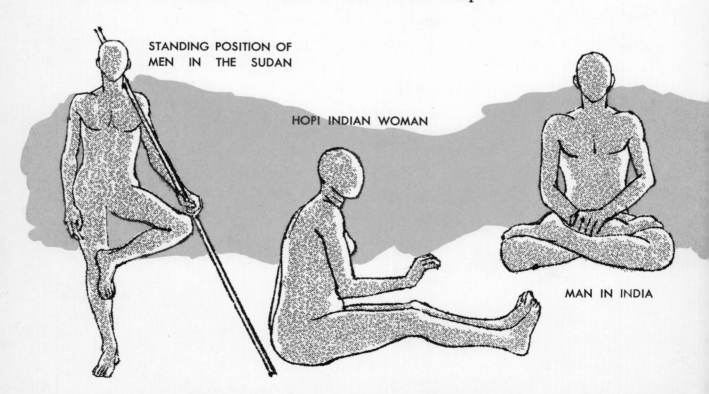

STANDING POSITION OF MEN IN THE SUDAN

HOPI INDIAN WOMAN

MAN IN INDIA

WHO INVENTED CHAIRS?

ABOUT FIVE THOUSAND years ago, Egyptians learned the art of joining pieces of wood together, and they made four-legged chairs. Before that, some people probably had three-legged stools. In parts of Africa, as far back as anyone knows, every man had a stool that was his own. When he left his house, his son carried his stool for him. The king of the Ashanti tribe had a golden stool.

But not all people in the world use chairs. Some prefer to sit on the floor or to squat on their heels. This may seem uncomfortable to you, if you are accustomed to chairs, but chairs do not suit those who have grown up without them. No one is born with a special habit of sitting or standing, for our bodies do not inherit knowledge of things our ancestors learned. We must learn such things for ourselves by watching others.

Scientists who study man and his ways have discovered that at least one-fourth of the people in the world never sit! Instead, they squat. The pictures show some of the most usual sitting positions.

Men are likely not to sit in the same way as women. Women often stretch their legs straight out in front of them on the floor. Or they may just cross their ankles. This seems to be the most comfortable position for holding a baby while a woman weaves or makes a basket or does other chores that men seldom do.

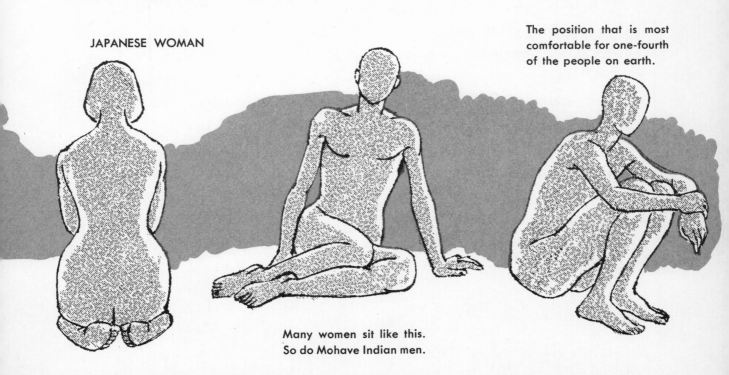

JAPANESE WOMAN

The position that is most comfortable for one-fourth of the people on earth.

Many women sit like this.
So do Mohave Indian men.

Sheep and goats could be kept by wandering people; but pigs are very independent and difficult to drive, so pigs were not tamed until men became settled farmers.

WHAT WAS THE FIRST ANIMAL THAT MEN TAMED?

LONG AGO, when people lived mostly by hunting, men and dogs formed a kind of partnership. Dogs, with their keen sense of smell, helped men to find wild game which men killed with spears. Both men and dogs had an easier time finding enough to eat when they worked together.

There was another possible reason for the partnership. When people had leftover food, dogs ate it. Men's waste helped to keep dogs alive, and dogs helped to clean up men's camps and caves.

No one knows the exact date when men and dogs got together. Possibly it was about eleven thousand years ago. Almost certainly, it was before people learned how to grow plants for food. Archeologists know that dogs had already been tamed about eight thousand years ago in the city of Jericho, in Jordan. By then, dogs were helping men to herd goats. This meant that goats had also been tamed at that time.

18

Chickens were first kept for their eggs in southeast Asia.

The reindeer that lived in northern Europe and Asia may have been herded by men a very long time ago, when the climate was colder than it is now. With a reindeer herd that could be kept together, people had a handy supply of meat for food and of skins for clothing. As time went on, they learned how to train the animals to pull sleds and carry loads.

Men used cattle on farms long before they used horses. An ox was strong, and it easily learned how to pull a cart or a plow. But horses were harder to control, and they could not work well in the kind of harness that was all right for oxen. This harness had a strap that went across the animal's throat. When the horse pulled, the strap cut off its breath. The harder it pulled, the more it was choked. Horse collars, invented in China, were not imported into Europe until about the ninth century, more than three thousand years after men had taught horses to pull light chariots.

19

A boy named Jonathan Leakey helped to discover the bones and tools of men who lived nearly 2,000,000 years ago. Working with his archeologist parents in Africa, Jonathan learned to recognize ancient human bones that appeared in places where a river had cut a canyon deep in the earth.

WHERE DID THE FIRST PEOPLE COME FROM?

MOST SCIENTISTS think that eastern Africa may be the place where the first true men appeared. Certainly the oldest human bones and tools that we know about were found buried deep in the earth in the East African country called Tanzania.

These earliest men lived about two million years ago. Their ancestors were manlike creatures that existed much longer ago than that.

While scientists are digging in the earth to find evidence of the first human beings, people everywhere continue to tell old stories that were made up to explain the great mystery of human life. Some American Indian tribes have tales about gods who molded the first man and woman from corn meal. The people of Babylon had a legend about a goddess who kneaded a bit of clay and turned it into a manlike creature. The ancient Hebrews borrowed some of this Babylonian story and added to it. They called the first human beings Adam and Eve. In Indonesia, it is believed that man hatched from an egg. Many, many tribes tell of creatures that came up from the ocean and turned into men. Sometimes we, too, say in fun that monkeys or apes came down out of the trees and turned into men. The fact is that long ago there lived an animal that was the ancestor of both apes and men. That animal is now extinct.

Although early men and apes were relatives, they were different in important ways. Men stood up straight and walked and ran on two legs. Human legs and ape legs were attached differently to the body, and the hip bones were not the same. Men's teeth were different, and so were the jaws in which the teeth grew. The biggest difference of all was in the brain: in man, the part of the brain used for talking and remembering was much bigger than in any ape.

Men and apes behave differently, too. Some apes can make very simple tools and use them on the spot where they need them. But an ape never makes a tool today which he intends to use tomorrow. Only man can think about the future and plan ahead. Only man can wonder about the past.

One of the early men in the world looked something like this. Archeologists call him Zinjanthropus. A scientific artist made the portrait with nothing but bones as a guide. The artist could tell how big the face muscles were and how they were shaped by studying the sizes and the locations of spots where muscles were attached to bones.

WHY ARE THERE SO MANY DIFFERENT KINDS OF PEOPLE IN THE WORLD?

WHEN YOU see pictures of the world's people, the first thought you have is: "How different they all look!" A scientist will agree with you. But then he will add: "They aren't nearly so different as they seem."

Every human being has a certain number of characteristics that he can pass along to his children. He has skin colour, hair texture, shape of eyes and nose and mouth. He has a stomach, lungs, fingers, toes, muscles, nerves. The list is very, very long. And when all the items on the list are added together, they show a surprising fact. Only one item out of every ten varies among normal people. We are all much more alike than we are different.

Still, the differences certainly do exist, and new ones can develop. Some scientists believe that differences between one group and another are most likely to appear when people live in small communities and don't marry any outsiders. For example, in Pennsylvania there are a few small settlements of people called Dunkers who have their own special religious

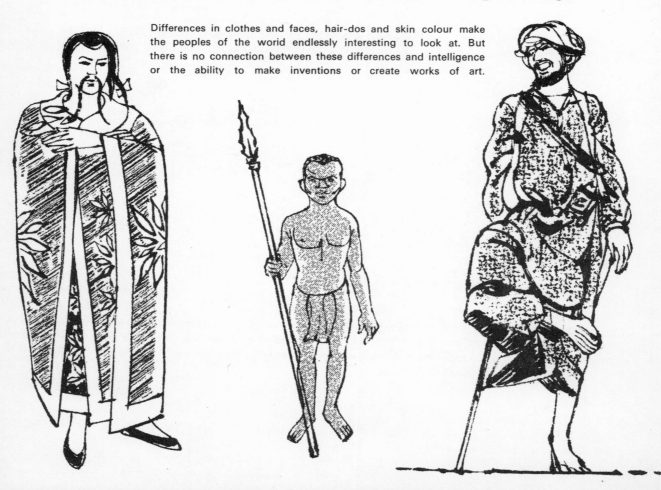

Differences in clothes and faces, hair-dos and skin colour make the peoples of the world endlessly interesting to look at. But there is no connection between these differences and intelligence or the ability to make inventions or create works of art.

faith. For about 250 years, members of the Dunker church have been marrying only Dunkers. In those 250 years, they have developed a combination of features that make them somewhat different from their non-Dunker neighbours. More often than not, they have straight thumbs; the lobes of their ears tend to be more dangling than those of other Pennsylvanians; they have less hair on the backs of their fingers.

This kind of thing has happened all over the world. Some scientists think that large groups called races may have grown out of small groups of people who did not let their members marry outsiders. Other scientists believe that climate may have been important, too. In sunny tropical countries, people with dark skin may have had a better chance of staying alive than people whose skins sunburned easily. That might be why dark-skinned people developed in New Guinea and Africa. On the other hand, people with very little coloring in their skins get along all right in the cloudier northern parts of the world where sunburn is not such a problem. And northern countries are where most of the light-skinned people have lived.

WHEN DID NAMES BEGIN?

SOME SCIENTISTS think that human beings have been talking for at least a million years. If this is true, people may have been using names for almost that long.

Very soon after men invented language, they began to feel that words in general and names in particular had a kind of magical power. They believed it was necessary to take special care of names, and various people worked out different ways of doing so. Some of these special customs are probably almost the same today as they were thousands of years ago. For example, in many places in the world people believe that once you have been given a name, it becomes part of you. Enemies can use it to harm you. It can lose strength and wear out if it is spoken too often, so real names are kept secret and nicknames are used instead. Many Navaho Indians have secret real names. When they go to school or have bank accounts or paint pictures, they sign their nicknames.

Some tribes in Australia never speak the name of a dead man for fear his ghost will hear it and come back to haunt them.

This Greek writer and philosopher is known only by his nickname. Perhaps it was because he had broad shoulders that he was always called "Broad." The Greek word for "broad" is *platon*, and Plato is what we call him today, more than two thousand years after his death.

24

Some people name new babies for ancestors who are dead, never for anyone who is living. Orthodox Jews follow this custom. Eskimos believe a name should be used only by one person at a time. When anyone dies, his name can go back into circulation, and a new baby can then have it.

The ancient Romans used nicknames. One man, even after he became emperor, was always called Caligula, which means "Little Boot." In Egypt, the nicknames of rulers were sometimes carved on stone in ancient tombs. In Japan, scholars used to give themselves pleasant-sounding nicknames, and today, writers and artists in America and Europe sometimes use nicknames as pen names.

The ceremony of naming children was a very important old custom. Sometimes a baby got only a temporary name, and as he grew older, he might be called several different things before he or his family settled on something permanent. But sometimes the fathers and mothers changed their names when children were born! As soon as the new baby had a name — such as Ahdem in Arabia, for example — the father was known only as Father-of-Ahdem.

WHY DO WE SAY "GOD BLESS YOU" WHEN SOMEONE SNEEZES?

Long, long ago, many people got the idea that there was a connection between names and sneezing. In some tribes, a ceremony was held for each new baby, and a priest would recite a whole list of names until at last the baby sneezed. That was supposed to show which name was his. Other tribes believed that when you sneezed, an enemy was using your name to do you harm. But if someone quickly said "God bless you," or "*Gesundheit*," which is German for "Good health," the words helped to protect your name from evil. We still say the words, although the belief that led to them has been forgotten.

So far as anyone knows, no English girls were called Florence until 1820. That year, a Mr. and Mrs. Nightingale gave their baby that name because she was born in the city of Florence, Italy. When she grew up, Florence Nightingale became the first English hospital nurse, and because of her great work, her first name became popular.

WHERE DO GIVEN NAMES COME FROM?

MOST NAMES have grown out of words that have meaning of some kind. Faith and Hope became popular in England during the time when a religious group called Puritans were trying to reform the official church. Some other Puritan names were Learn-Wisdom, Hate-Evil, Search-the-Scriptures. One man was called Praise-God Barebones, and he had a brother who was known as Damned. This was short for If-Christ-Had-Not-Died-For-Thee-Thou-Wouldst-Have-Been-Damned Barebones.

Many Puritans moved to America seeking freedom to worship as they wanted to, and they carried with them their name-making customs. Puritan names lasted much longer in America than in England.

In the days when Christianity was a new religion, men and women who joined it were given new names. This was called *christening* in English. Later, the phrase *christened name* was pronounced *Christian name*. Now the term is often used to mean simply a person's given name, whether he is a Christian or not.

26

Mary, the most popular girl's name in the United States, comes from the Hebrew word that means bitterness. Many people in Christian countries use it to show their belief that Mary was the Mother of Jesus. John, one of the most popular of boys' names, also comes from a Hebrew word. In one form or another, it is used in many countries: Jean is the French form; Jan is the Dutch; Ivan is the Russian.

Sometimes, parents want to give a child an unusual name, and so they make up a new one. For some reason, many white people in Oklahoma have made-up names such as Zazelle, Rulema, Juhree for girls; Raysal and Moneer for boys.

WHERE DO MIDDLE NAMES COME FROM?

THE FIRST known middle name in England appeared in 1363. It belonged to a man called John Philip Capel. The fashion of using middle names apparently came to England from France, and the French took the custom from Spain. Perhaps it was started there by parents who thought that if it helped a child to have one name that had belonged to a saint, it would help him more if he had two or more saints' names.

The three-name custom was slow to reach Protestant America. Before the American Revolution, almost nobody had a middle name, but today, most people in the United States do. Sometimes, if a man is not given one by his parents, he makes it up or he may just use a middle initial. Because of a family disagreement over Shippe or Solomon (after names of two grandfathers), President Harry S. Truman used only the letter S. for his middle name. A famous cave explorer and professor of geology is Harlan J Bretz. The middle name is simply the letter J without a full-stop after it.

A Russian often gets his middle name as well as his last name from his father. The middle one is the father's first name with an ending that means *son of*. For example, Nikita Sergeivich Khrushchev, means Nikita, the son of Sergei Khrushchev.

WHY DO PEOPLE HAVE FAMILY NAMES?

"I AM MYSELF and not somebody else." That is what a name says.

If you live in a small group, one name is enough to keep you distinct from others. But in a large group, several people may have the same name, and then there will be mix-ups. An extra name helps. You probably have an extra name that belongs to your whole family.

The Chinese seem to have been the first to use family names. They had the idea several thousand years ago. Later, the Romans had the same idea. Officials of the Roman Empire travelled about a great deal, meeting many people, and they discovered that it was easier to remember who was who if everybody had two names or even three. Family names came to be widely used by the Romans, but finally, the Roman Empire ended and for a long time there was very little travel anywhere in Europe. People went back to living in small separate groups. The need for family names disappeared.

Then, about A.D. 1000, Frenchmen began to move around a little more. Owners of large estates wanted some way of identifying themselves. They added the names of their estates to their given names. Soon, the name of an estate became the name of the family that owned it.

When the French invaded England in 1066, they took this custom with them. All over England, the name of a place became the name of the noble family who lived there. Later, the people who managed the

28

estate adopted the idea. Finally, the poor began to get family names, too. At that time, nearly two million people lived in England, but they used only about twenty given names for boys and twenty for girls. Since the officials who collected rent and taxes were eager to tell one John or one William from another, they made sure that the two-name custom spread.

In England today, there are more than 40,000 different family names. In the United States, the number is very great because people from almost every country in the world settled in this new land and brought their names with them. One expert estimates there are 350,000 different family names in the United States.

But not everybody who comes to a new land keeps his old name. Often his neighbours find it too hard to pronounce. That happened to a Frenchman who moved to Boston when Massachusetts was still a British colony. Other Bostonians had trouble with his name, Appolas Rivoire, so he changed it to Paul Revere. His son, also Paul Revere, made a famous ride on horseback at the time of the American Revolution to warn his countrymen that British soldiers were coming.

Many Negro people in the United States get their last names from the men who owned their ancestors as slaves. Some, who feel angry because they have been cut off from the real names of their real ancestors, have given up the family names they got from slaveholders. They have adopted new names in protest. Some simply call themselves by a number, such as Ali 3, or by a letter, such as Malcolm X.

WHERE DO FAMILY NAMES COME FROM?

ORIGINALLY, family names in China came from a sacred poem that has 438 different words. This means that there could be only 438 different family names for millions of Chinese people. Each Chinese family also had a special poem of its own with twenty or thirty characters in it, and from these words came a person's middle name. In addition, everyone had a given name called a *milk name*. Usually, the family name was written first, then the second name, then the milk name. So a famous Chinese leader called Sun Yat Sen was Mr. Sun.

Common people in England often got their names from the work they did: Baker, Powdermaker, Cooper (a man who makes barrels). Men also took names from the places where they lived or from some feature of the landscape nearby — for example, Westfield, Shore, Hill.

For thousands of years, people who followed the Jewish religion had no regular family names. A boy named Isaac might be called Isaac ben Jacob, but that merely meant he was the son of Jacob. Then, about 150 years ago, the Christian governments of countries in eastern Europe made laws requiring Jews to choose family names. But in many places, Jews were forbidden to take any names that Christians were already

using, and so they had to make up new ones. Often, they put together words that suggested things of beauty: flower mountain (Blumberg), rose valley (Rosenthal), gold stone (Goldstein).

In Austria, government officials began to charge a fee for suggesting a name. The more attractive it was, the higher the fee. If an Austrian could not afford to pay much, he got a name that was not very desirable, and very poor people sometimes were given names that sounded silly or unpleasant.

The most popular of all Jewish family names has a different history. It comes from a word that means *priest*. The usual way of spelling this name in the English-speaking world is Cohen. But if the family came from Germany, it may be spelled Kahn or Kohn. A Kagan or a Kahan probably came originally from Russia.

In Spanish-speaking countries, a woman keeps her own name after she marries. Her son may choose either her name or his father's, or he may combine them, putting the letter *y* between the two. *Y* in Spanish means *and*. So Juan Rivera y Gonzalez means: John, the son of Mr. Rivera and his wife who was born into a family called Gonzales.

Boys learn to
dance in Brazil.

WHEN WAS THE FIRST SCHOOL STARTED?

ALMOST ALL the children ever born in the world have wanted to learn how to share in grown-up life. Parents have always taught them skills and songs and dances, beliefs and manners. So, in a way, there have been schools as long as there have been people.

In the very beginning, men taught boys how to make tools and weapons out of stone. Women taught girls to gather seeds and to grind them so they were easier to eat. As time went on, boys and girls had a great deal of special learning to do before they were considered grown-up. They had to learn the ceremonies and legends of their people, as well as practical everyday skills.

We don't know exactly how teaching was done tens of thousands of years ago, but we do know that it went on all the time. One very old art school has been discovered. In a cave in France, archeologists have found practice drawings on bits of stone. Student artists apparently made these sketches before they worked on bigger drawings on the cave walls, and a teacher corrected the sketches. He showed beginners how to improve their work. The skilled lines made by the teacher can be seen very clearly on top of the clumsy lines made by beginners on the bits of stone.

Although nobody can say for sure, it is probable that teachers seldom spanked their pupils in these very early schools, and parents did not often strike a child as they tried to teach him all the things he had to know. At that time, there were no powerful rulers who expected everyone else to obey orders, and parents themselves did not use force. Physical punishment for children did not come until dictatorial governments demanded obedience from common people. In the ancient land of Sumer, for example, leaders governed by force, and teachers had whipping switches to use on pupils who were slow with their lessons.

In many ancient schools, students did almost nothing but memorize, and they worked out all kinds of tricks for remembering lessons. No method is stranger than the one still used by boys in Morocco. They eat roasted and powdered hedgehog liver which they believe will help them to remember.

In other African schools, teachers believe it is important for children to learn how to think. So they use riddles to sharpen their pupils' wits. Many of the riddles are very, very hard, but here are two that you can probably figure out:

A little white hut that has no door. What is it? (An egg.)

Mother is tiny, but she makes good food. Who is she? (A bee.)

A music class in Morocco. Only recently have Moroccan girls been allowed to go to school.

WHERE DO MANNERS COME FROM?

IN MANY PARTS of the world, men shake hands when they meet. Long ago, this custom may have started as a way of showing that they were not holding weapons. Whatever notion once lay behind a handshake, men don't think about it nowadays. They are just being polite or friendly.

When two Americans meet — or two Britons — they give each other a firm grip. But that particular kind of handshake would not be considered good manners by Navaho Indians or by Somalis in Africa. A Navaho or a Somali just holds a hand out limply and touches the friend's hand, which should also be limp. A man in Laos behaves differently. He is not being polite unless he gives a really strong vigorous shake. Frenchmen are likely to shake hands very often — when they meet, when they part, just before every meal. Englishmen make less of the custom. In ancient China, when two men met, each shook his *own* two hands.

Other ways of being polite have just as many variations. In ancient Egypt, a young person showed his respect for old people by rising when they came near — just as many modern young people do. In another part of Africa today, the young always crouch down when the old approach.

Etiquette is another name for good manners or proper behavior. In the beginning, this French word meant a ticket that ordinary people were given when they were to be introduced to the king. Rules printed on it explained how one behaved when among royalty — where to stand and what to do. After the French people revolted against their king in 1789, this kind of etiquette disappeared for a while. Then a man named Napoleon, who did not come from a noble family, made himself emperor. Very soon, Napoleon put together a huge *Book of Ceremonial* filled with rules and regulations from former times. The book told how to do practically everything — even how to fold a letter. Napoleon thought that all this etiquette was necessary in order to make the French people believe he was a royal personage who really deserved respect and obedience.

In Mongolia, where the climate is very dry, the polite way to greet a man is to ask: "Has the rain fallen in your neighbourhood?" But in Poland, where it rains often, farmers always used to ask: "Is it too wet?" English-speaking people are likely to say: "How do you do?" The age-old greeting in the Soviet Republic of Georgia is, "Victory to you!"

Rules for politeness surround all of us all through life. Often a particular custom does not have much meaning by itself, but all of them have one thing in common: They help to bring order into people's lives. Good manners mean that you know what to do and what to expect of others. The rules help you to get along with your fellow man, and that makes living much more pleasant.

Rules about manners also help whole countries to get along with each other. Many governments even have special employees whose job it is to see that important officials and foreign guests are seated in the right places at dinners, are introduced in the proper order, and so on. If the employee isn't sure what is correct, he can usually find out by looking in a special book.

People need to have some kind of order, no matter whether they live in small groups or big ones. Of course, manners aren't the main thing in life, any more than oil is the main thing in an automobile engine, but both manners and oil keep things running smoothly.

WHY DO MEN RAISE THEIR HATS?

THE CUSTOM of uncovering one's head as a gesture of politeness is very old. In ancient Rome, during cold weather, men wore big robes with loose ends that could be pulled up over the head for warmth. When a man met a friend, he didn't want to appear to be hiding, so he uncovered his head. Later, during the Middle Ages, when knights often wore armour and helmets, they had a similar way of showing peaceful intentions. If a knight met a friend, he lifted his visor. This uncovered his face. Indoors, he removed the entire helmet.

Still later, when men gave up helmets and began to wear hats instead, they continued the friendly gesture of uncovering when they met people they knew.

In many countries today, men usually take off their hats when they enter houses or offices or lifts. It is a custom in most Christian churches for men to bare their heads. But Jews and Moslems always wear hats or other head coverings during religious services. This custom is much older than the Christian custom based on the habits of knights in the Middle Ages.

WHY DO SOLDIERS SALUTE?

THIS CUSTOM, like doffing hats, dates from the days when knights raised their visors as a gesture of friendship and respect. Among soldiers, the raising of the right hand to the forehead continued after the helmet and the visor disappeared.

WHY DO SOLDIERS START MARCHING WITH THE LEFT FOOT?

MORE THAN two thousand years ago, Greek warriors carried their shields in the left hand, and so the left side was turned toward the enemy when they went into battle. The habit that came from advancing with the shield on the left side continued after shields were no longer used. That is why soldiers still start marching with the left foot.

HOW DID TABLE MANNERS BEGIN?

PEOPLE had table manners before they had tables. For thousands of years, they sat on the ground and the host and his guests all ate from one large dish or pot or tray. Each group had its own rules about the proper way to behave so that everybody would feel comfortable at meals and receive what was considered a fair share of the food.

Certain eating customs spread widely over the world, and they changed very little as time passed. In Iran, for example, villagers still gather around a central dish or tray on the floor. Everyone — out of respect for the others — washes before eating and then takes food only with the right hand, which is supposed to be the clean hand. Each person dips into the side of the tray nearest to him. He never watches another person eat. All during the meal, he remains in a kneeling position because that is what the prophet Mohammed is supposed to have done to show his sympathy for slaves who had to kneel before their masters. When an Iranian finishes eating, it is good manners for him to lick his fingers.

In Mongolia, a polite person licks the bowl from which he has eaten. Each guest in a Mongolian tent is given a bowl of his own, which often contains tea flavoured with butter.

Eskimos, and some South Sea Islanders, have a different way of being polite at the end of the meal. They belch, which for them is the same as saying: "Thank you, the food was excellent." Many other people think belching is bad manners. Indeed, in some places any sound at meals is impolite. One of the first European books on table manners said: "Do not make a sucking noise while you take food from your spoon." This was written by an Italian in the thirteenth century. Another old book by a Frenchman said: "Do not blow on soup in order to cool it. . . . Do not talk with your mouth full. . . . Do not carry fruit away from the table in your pocket."

On the other hand, an ancient Roman host felt insulted if guests failed to take fruit home. He even gave them little squares of cloth to wrap it in. Perhaps those squares were the first table napkins, but if so, the custom of using them died out for hundreds of years. In northern

Europe, even at royal banquets, guests wiped their hands on the table-cloths, which weren't washed very often.

European kings themselves didn't begin to have table napkins until the 1500's, when Henry VIII ruled England. From his dining room, the custom spread to the homes of noblemen, and then, about two hundred years ago, to the homes of ordinary people. At that time, something new happened. Weaving machines in factories began to produce cheap cloth, and the incomes of ordinary men increased. So the use of table napkins could spread. During that same period, an Englishman named Josiah Wedgwood began to manufacture lots of cheap sets of dishes. Until then, only the rich could afford enough plates and bowls to go around; other people often ate out of a common bowl. Wedgwood and the cloth factories were responsible for a big change in table manners.

Japanese people think it is impolite to talk very much at meals. So do Chinese, Maoris, and others. Cowboys in the Old West seldom had much to say while they were eating. But long ago, the Egyptians thought it was rude not to carry on a conversation at the dinner table. French people think so today. In old Poland, everyone talked, but never about the food, and it was very impolite to act as if you were hungry.

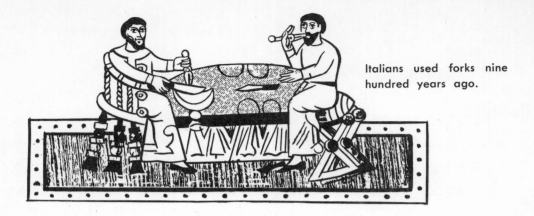

Italians used forks nine hundred years ago.

WHEN WERE KNIVES AND FORKS INVENTED?

STONE KNIVES were one of man's earliest inventions. Spoons are very ancient, too. But people had been using them for thousands of years before anyone thought of making table forks. Knives were carried around, stuck into the belt or the boot top. When large portions of meat came to the table, a man took out his knife, cut off what he wanted, and ate it with his fingers.

Turkey and other Eastern countries had forks before Europe did. No one is sure how long ago Asians began to eat with forks, but the custom did not spread to Italy until after A.D. 1000. It reached England still later. In fact, Englishmen who visited Italy in the Middle Ages made fun of the men they saw spearing food daintily with forks after it had been cut up for them in the kitchen.

King Henry VIII was the first Englishman to adopt the Italian custom. He had three forks to choose from. His daughter, Queen Elizabeth I, had a larger collection. But most people used only knives and spoons at table until about the year 1700. A great many Americans had no forks at the time of the American Revolution.

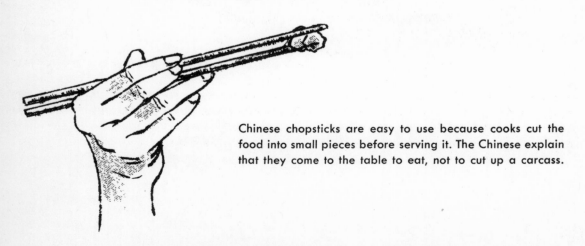

Chinese chopsticks are easy to use because cooks cut the food into small pieces before serving it. The Chinese explain that they come to the table to eat, not to cut up a carcass.

HOW DID PEOPLE FIND OUT WHAT IS GOOD TO EAT?

NOBODY KNOWS what foods the first people chose — or why. Fish bones have been found along with some very ancient tools, and it seems likely that early men were able to eat both plant food and meat. Many other creatures had to be either plant-eaters or meat-eaters. They could digest only one kind of food. Men were more flexible. They could experiment.

Of course, there were real dangers in experimenting. Many berries, roots and mushrooms were poisonous. But at times men had to try new things or starve. Their customary foods became scarce, or they moved to new territory where they could not find the foods they were used to. Gradually, out of necessity — and out of daring, too — the world's foods came to be known. Every important plant, animal, fish and bird that we eat today was discovered by some prehistoric tribe somewhere.

One widely used food is an amazing invention. It comes from the root of the bitter cassava plant, which is very poisonous if you eat it raw. But if you pound the root, squeeze out the juice, and wash the pulp, you get a starchy substance that makes nourishing bread. The juice itself can be boiled down into a delicious and harmless sauce.

About two hundred years ago, the Zulu tribe in Africa moved into new territory and drove out the people who were living there. These refugees later told what happened. In their new home, they learned about some new foods by observing what the animals ate safely. They experimented with other foods that sometimes made them sick, but by trial and error, they managed to get enough to eat.

WHY DO PEOPLE EAT SOME FOODS BUT NOT OTHERS?

WOULD YOU eat grasshoppers or mice or snakes or dogs? Probably not, but some people do — and they like the taste. The same thing is true of horses and cats and caterpillars. On the other hand, food that you think is delicious may seem disgusting to certain people. For instance, the very thought of drinking milk can make an old-fashioned Chinese feel sick. But this same Chinese would consider pork a great delicacy, although no Orthodox Jew or Moslem would touch it.

Orthodox Jews won't eat any meat unless all the blood is drained out of it, but some Africans raise cattle mainly because they drink the blood. They have found ways of taking this nourishing food from living animals without doing them harm.

A strict Navaho man will never eat eggs or fish. Eskimos eat both fish and meat, but almost no plant food. Some American Indian tribes — and tribes of Armenia — depended mainly on meat. They looked down on plant-eaters, and even today, long after they have ceased to live by hunting or herding, they don't care to learn the arts of growing vegetables and grain.

DINNER IN INDIA

AN ARAB FEAST

People often think they avoid a certain food because something about it is unwholesome, and sometimes there really is a practical reason for being careful. Certain plants are poisonous.

Usually, though, people are "taught" in early childhood to like some foods and to avoid others. Often this teaching has little to do with whether a food is wholesome and nourishing.

Many notions about foods go back to an ancient belief in magic. For reasons that nobody remembers, prehistoric tribesmen came to think that a powerful spirit would be offended if they ate a certain thing. The spirit would do harm if its wishes were ignored. Today, scientists have a word for the things people believe they must not eat or do. These things are said to be *taboo*. The word comes from a South Sea Island where *taboo* means forbidden.

In many places, foods that were once taboo are now eaten. Fashions in foods change, too. In New York, for example, one can buy chocolate-covered ants, roasted grasshoppers, and canned rattlesnake meat.

A Japanese bride wears a headdress. So does a Moslem bride in Sumatra, and a parasol is carried over her head. Many European and American women wear wedding veils, just as women did in ancient Greece. During Jewish ceremonies a canopy is held over both bride and groom. All of these customs at weddings are very old. In ancient times, head-covering was believed to protect the couple from evil.

HOW DID PEOPLE GET MARRIED IN THE OLD DAYS?

WHEN ENGLISH-SPEAKING people get married, they say they have a wedding. A wedding usually is a ceremony for the marriage of a man and woman who have fallen in love with each other. But in the old days, the word *wed* had quite a different meaning. Love, in ancient times in England, had nothing to do with getting married. Instead, marriages were arranged by parents — often when a boy and girl were babies. The *wed* was a sum of money that the boy's parents paid to the girl's parents as a guarantee that the marriage would really take place when the children grew up.

Parents in many places still arrange marriages. In Japan, some families allow young people to choose for themselves, but parents often hire a matchmaker who finds husbands or wives for their children. Most peoples of the world have rules telling who can marry whom. This custom is very old, and some of the rules are very complicated. In Australia, for example, an Arunta man is not supposed to get married until he has found a bride who is his mother's mother's brother's daughter's daughter.

The idea that a man should have only one wife at a time seems sensible to people brought up in Europe and in America. But there are many stories in the Bible about men who had several wives. Those who practice the religion called Islam (Moslems) believe a man may have four wives, and so do some African tribes. There have also been groups of people who believed that it was sensible for a woman to have several husbands. One such group lived in Tibet.

No matter what their beliefs are, almost all people hold wedding ceremonies. Those who belong to Christian churches often get married in June. This custom started long ago in ancient Rome. The month of June was sacred to Juno, who was the Romans' goddess of marriage, and people thought she would be likely to give happiness and good luck to a couple married in her month.

Wedding ceremonies change from time to time, and each group has its own customs, but one thing remains just about the same: it is usually the job of families to take care of children.

WHY ARE SOME PEOPLE MORE CIVILIZED THAN OTHERS?

FIVE THOUSAND years ago, the people in northern Europe had only crude tools made of stone, and they got their food by hunting wild animals. At this same time, some of the people in Africa and Asia knew how to make tools of metal, and kept herds of tame animals and raised crops.

Not a single blond northerner knew how to read or write at a time when kings in Egypt and priests in the Asian land of Sumer were making written records of their wealth and their ideas. The fact that these groups belonged to different races had nothing to do with their abilities, however. Britons and other northern tribesmen remained uncivilized for a longer time than did many Africans and Asians, but not because they were stupid. They simply lived in the wrong place. They were too far away from points where the uses of metal were discovered, where farming began, and where people did a great deal of trading with each other. Only a little trade went on in northern Europe five thousand years ago. Even two thousand years ago, there was very little long-distance travel. This meant that people in one tribe knew little about faraway tribes. When different people do not meet, it is hard for them to learn from each other.

The blond tribes of northern Europe could not become skilled in art, in science and in business until they had learned from southerners how to save energy by using metal tools, and how to grow quantities of

energy-producing food. This knowledge came gradually as farmers from the south moved northward looking for new fields to cultivate. Slowly, most of Europe mastered the art of raising grain and caring for cattle and sheep. Traders introduced new products and new ideas — especially from Asia. The once-uncivilized nations began to catch up. Then the New World was discovered. From that time on, trade increased quickly in northern Europe. So did inventions and scientific discoveries and learning. People who had been on the outer fringe of civilization now found themselves at its very centre.

Today, some people still live in very old-fashioned ways, ways that keep them poor in a world where others are comfortable and rich. The reason is not that they are stupid or foolish, any more than the Britons were stupid in ancient times. Almost always, these people have somehow been kept from meeting people with ideas that are different from their own. Some of them live in jungles or desert country. Others have ancient customs that conflict with modern efficient ways of doing things. Some have not been allowed by conquerors to have opportunities to learn.

Very often, one group has called others uncivilized when they were only different. More than two thousand years ago, Greeks scorned others who did not speak their language. Foreigners, they said, sounded as if they mumbled only, *"Bar-bar-bar."* The English word *barbarian,* meaning an uncivilized person, comes from this haughty Greek term for people who were different.

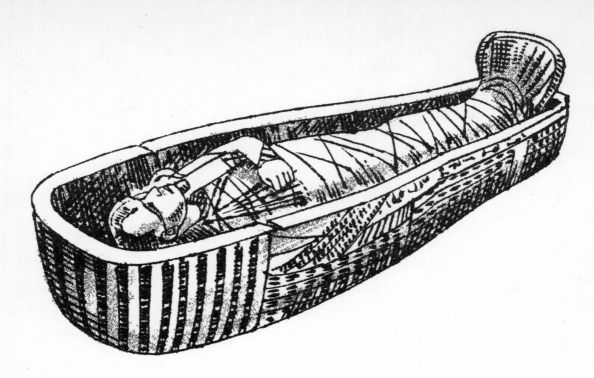

WHY DID THE EGYPTIANS MAKE MUMMIES?

ANCIENT EGYPTIANS believed that when a person went to sleep, his soul left his body. When the soul returned to the body, he woke up. When he died, the soul went away for a long stay. But sooner or later, it would want to return, and this belief meant that bodies had to be preserved. It led to the making of mummies.

The practice of mummification started with the rich kings and later spread downward to the poor people. When the custom became general, the embalmers had a great deal of work to do. Knowledge of how to do it was passed along from father to son in certain families, and many different ways of preserving bodies were developed. Those who could afford the most expensive funerals had their bodies wrapped in strips of linen especially woven for the purpose. On each strip was written a prayer or magic spell that was supposed to help make sure the mummy would be safe and ready when the soul wanted to rejoin it.

In the beginning, bodies were sometimes buried in the hot sand of the desert. There they dried out and were preserved. Later, embalmers used various spices or cedar oil or salt or honey.

Certain animals in Egypt were sacred, and they had special protection inside temple grounds. When one of them died, it was mummified and buried in an animal cemetery. Many bull and cat mummies, and even some mummified crocodiles and fish, have been found.

The Egyptians took such interest in a future life that they built huge tombs for their kings. Some of the tombs were in the form of pyramids, and the men who designed them had to develop great skill as engineers and mathematicians.

WHY DID MEN WEAR WIGS LONG AGO?

THE FIRST WIG was probably made for a ruler who was bald, but thought he would look better with hair. Five hundred years ago wigs for noblemen were fashionable in Italy. At that same time, Italian peasant women wore their hair short. They cut it to sell to wig-makers in the cities.

Most men in France at about that time had long hair, although they did not wear wigs. Then the king hurt his head and had to have his hair cut. Immediately, noblemen began cutting theirs, too. But the next thing they knew, another king came to the throne, and he had a great mop of naturally curly hair. This started a new fad. Noblemen began to have big curly wigs made.

In England, King Henry VIII made it a law that all men must wear short hair, but could have moustaches and beards as big as they liked. In later times, English kings allowed the wearing of wigs. It wasn't until the nineteenth century that men in Europe adopted a fairly uniform kind of short haircut. Even then, lawyers and judges continued to wear curled wigs. They still do in England and in a few other countries. The wigs are a symbol reminding everyone to respect the law.

Egyptian metalworkers are pouring hot liquid bronze into moulds. They use two bent sticks to protect their hands. Another man carries a piece of copper shaped like an ox-hide. Copper money had this shape in many places, probably because ox-hides were a kind of money in earlier times.

HOW DID MEN DISCOVER METALS?

IF YOU visit an iron mine or a copper mine, all you will see is rock. There will be no sign of metal. You would never suspect that such rock can be turned into material for wires, bells, swords or hoes. So it is no wonder that men had no metal tools for hundreds of thousands of years. However, men did learn to make very good use of stone. With great skill, they could strike two rocks together so that one would break and form a sharp cutting edge.

As toolmakers searched along river beds for the right kinds of stone, they sometimes found little yellow pebbles. These did not break when they were pounded. Instead, they flattened out. The yellow pebbles were really nuggets of gold, and in time men learned to hammer and shape the unusual stuff into ornaments. Gold was the first metal that some people used, because they happened to find it in pure chunks, unmixed with any other minerals.

In many places lumps of pure copper were discovered first. Like gold nuggets, they were soft enough to be hammered out into sheets, but they, too, were scarce.

In the search for metal nuggets and other useful materials, people found certain blue and green rocks that made beautiful paints when they were pounded into a fine powder and mixed with oils. Members of many tribes decorated their bodies with coloured paints, and Egyptian women used them for eye shadow, just as modern women do, but no one had any idea that there was a connection between the blue and green paints and reddish copper metal.

Finally, one day someone must have dropped a chunk of the coloured rock onto glowing charcoal in an extremely hot fire — perhaps in one of the ovens in which pottery was baked. A surprising thing happened. The rock which we call ore was changed by the heat, and out came melted copper!

Here were two discoveries in one. Copper could be obtained from a certain kind of rock, and when the metal was hot enough, it became liquid. It could be poured. If a man let hot liquid copper run into a knife-shaped mould, the metal would cool and harden into a knife.

Copper tools made in this way were soft, and for many jobs the old hard stone ones worked better. But very soon, probably by chance, someone combined tin ore with a copper ore in a hot fire. A mixture of copper and tin came out, and this mixture, called bronze, was hard. A bronze tool stayed sharp for a long time, and it did not break as easily as stone did. Moreover, when it got dull, the bronze could be melted down and used again in a new tool.

Presently, men began heating all kinds of rock to see what would happen. Often they got no metals at all from their experiments. But they did discover silver, lead, tin and iron. Iron was not good for much at first. It broke easily. But at last, after hundreds of years, metalworkers discovered ways of making iron into a very tough material that was both useful and cheap.

With plenty of iron tools and weapons, the lives of human beings changed a great deal. The country around them changed, too, and for a special reason. Whole huge forests had to be cut down and the wood turned into charcoal which produced the great heat needed to make good iron. At first, ironworkers used stone axes to chop down trees. Then with the help of the new iron axes, they could cut more wood much faster. By this time, men had learned to raise crops, and as the forests disappeared, fields were often planted in their place. More farms meant more food, particularly when farmers sped up their work by using iron tools. And with more food, there could be still more people to grow still more food — all because of iron.

WHEN DID MINING BEGIN?

METAL MINING began with the search for rock that could be heated and made into copper. It went on to become a search for other metals. In fact, the very word *metal* comes from a Greek word meaning *to search*.

At first, men looked for the right rocks only on the surface of the ground. Then they began to dig down into the earth. By 3000 B.C., they were taking ore from underground mines in the country we now call Israel. Later, King Solomon got copper ore from these mines. There were also very ancient Egyptian mines in a place called Sinai. A poem in the Book of Job in the Bible tells how these mines were worked: "Iron is taken out of the earth, and copper is smelted from ore. Men put an end to darkness, and search out the ore in gloom and deep darkness. They open shafts in a valley away from where men live . . . As for earth, out of it comes bread; but underneath it is turned up by fire . . . Man puts his hand to the flinty rock, and overturns mountains by the roots. He cuts out channels in the rocks, and his eye sees every precious thing . . . and the thing that is hid he brings forth to light."

Those words were probably written about four hundred years before Christ, but they describe the way mines had been worked for a long time. When the poet says the earth was turned up by fire, he means that miners built fires in the underground tunnels to heat the rock and make it split. Water poured on the hot rock sometimes helped to break it up.

Chinese metalworkers are said to have melted copper and iron in fires made with coal about three thousand years ago, but in Europe there were no great coal mines until the twelfth century. Then blacksmiths began burning it in their shops, and it was also used to heat big kettles of dye for clothmakers. The smell of the smoke annoyed people, and for a while, French blacksmiths were forbidden by law to burn coal.

WHAT WAS THE STONE AGE?

THE STORY of mankind can be divided into large chapters which are named for the materials from which people made their tools. First came stone tools, and the period in which men used them is called the Stone Age. It began perhaps two million years ago, and it has not yet ended for certain tribes. In parts of Australia, New Guinea and South Africa, men still make their spears and hammers and knives of stone.

Often this first and longest chapter in history is divided into the Old Stone Age, the Middle Stone Age, and the New Stone Age. In many places the New Stone Age began about nine thousand years ago, when men first learned to raise crops. The farmers of the New Stone Age had no sharp cutting instruments made of metal, and they did not get any until they learned about copper and bronze.

WHEN DID THE BRONZE AGE BEGIN?

IN THE PART of Asia that is called the Near East the Bronze Age began about 3000 B.C. In other places it began later. It lasted until craftsmen discovered that a certain kind of hardened iron was better — and cheaper. The arts of metalworking spread gradually all over Europe. In some places the Bronze Age was very short, because knowledge of iron came along soon after men had learned how to make bronze.

Africans in Nubia became famous as iron-makers more than two thousand years ago. The tribesmen who now live there still make iron in the kind of furnaces their ancestors used.

DO WE STILL LIVE IN THE IRON AGE?

THE IRON AGE began when blacksmiths discovered a very important new way to make weapons and tools of iron. First, the smith heated a lump of the metal in a charcoal fire. Then he pounded it into shape and heated it again. As if by magic, an ordinary brittle piece of iron grew tough and hard — very good for knives and swords. This process is called steeling, and it made iron into a widely useful material for the first time.

Steeling was apparently discovered by tribesmen in Armenia sometime before 1500 B.C. Then people called Hittites conquered the Armenians and learned about steeling but kept it secret. For more than two hundred years, the Hittites used weapons of the hardened iron to build a great empire. Finally, the secret leaked out. Men in Africa, Asia and Europe began to make good new weapons and tools. In all these places, the Iron Age began with the knowledge of how to harden iron.

Since iron is such an important metal, we can say that we still live in the Iron Age. But in some books you will find the end of the Iron Age given as 50 B.C. This simply means that by then iron tools had become well established in much of Europe. Of course, there were still people in the world who used tools of stone and bronze. But they were not the ones who played the most important part in later history.

HOW DO SUPERSTITIONS GET STARTED?

ONE DAY, an Eskimo hunter waited for hours without catching so much as a glimpse of a seal. At last, he grew hungry and went home for a bone to chew on. No sooner had he come back than a seal appeared, and he speared it. The hunter's bone seemed to have attracted the animal. After that, he always carried a bone along when he went hunting, and he said it always brought him luck.

Of course, a modern scientist would say that this was coincidence. Bone does not really attract seals. But it is the sort of thing that has often started a superstition among people who did not know anything about science.

After superstitions begin, they are likely to spread. If a father assures his son that it is lucky to see a white horse, the child accepts the notion and in time tells it to *his* children. If a chief, a priest, or anyone in authority passes the belief along, almost everybody will think it is true, and it will gradually travel far and wide. The belief that a white horse brings good luck must be a very old one, for it can be found in many widely separated parts of the world.

Dreams have probably started some superstitions. When a dream is very clear and sharp, it can seem as real as an actual event. A man who might have dreamed that he had a bad time with a black cat could easily connect it with bad luck from then on. Fears can also turn into beliefs that travel from person to person.

Sometimes a real experience can turn into a superstition. For example, many people think it is bad luck to spill salt. This belief goes back to the days when salt was so precious that any loss of it might truly cause hardship. Men did not particularly need salt as long as they were hunters, because they lived on the meat of animals that licked salt from the earth. But then, farming began. People lived mainly on cereals that contained so little salt that farmers had to add it to their food. In some places it was very scarce and expensive. To spill it was a real misfortune.

Today, even in places where salt is cheap, the old fear lingers on as a superstition, and a new superstition has been added to it. "You can avoid the bad luck," it is said, "if you throw a bit of the spilled salt over your left shoulder."

Many people have superstitions about left and right. In some places, their beliefs grew out of a kind of fortune-telling that was taken very seriously. What was going to happen in the future? Would a war or a business deal be successful? Men tried to find answers by magic, and they came to believe that nature could give them signs and signals. For example, if birds flew to the left, it meant one thing; to the right, another. Our word *sinister,* which means *threatening,* is the old Roman word for *left.*

WHY DO WE CALL UNEXPECTED MONEY A WINDFALL?

WHEN A PERSON gets a valuable prize or wins money in a lottery, he may say he has had a *windfall.* This word has meant good luck ever since the eleventh century, when William the Conqueror ruled England. At that time, the king and the lords wanted to protect the forests they owned, and so they made it a crime for a peasant to cut down a tree. However, it was all right for him to use any tree that the wind had blown down. In time, a tree that had been blown over became known as a windfall. To a poor peasant, a windfall was a stroke of very good luck.

WAS THERE A REAL ROBIN HOOD?

IN BRITAIN there is a very old belief in fairies and little folk who came out of the woods and helped children or poor people in trouble. There may be a bit of truth in the belief. Some historians think that the first inhabitants of Britain really were quite small, shy people. When bold warriors from Europe invaded their island, they retreated into the forests. Little bands of them may have lived on, scarcely seen, for a long, long time. Legends about them grew and transformed them into fairies who worked wonders for the poor.

In the fourteenth century, and perhaps earlier, the leader of the magic band was called Robin, and he wore a green hood — just as fairies and gnomes did. So, Robin à Hood, or Robin Hood, became the hero's name. He and his followers numbered thirteen, altogether — exactly as many as bands of witches were supposed to have.

Probably no one person was the real Robin Hood. But there were many real people who lived in the woods and fought a kind of guerilla war against the rich and powerful lords. In the Robin Hood legends, these true stories and the old folk tales got thoroughly mixed together.

WHY DO PEOPLE SAY A CAT HAS 9 LIVES?

THIS SAYING goes back to the ancient Egyptians, who worshipped cats. The Egyptians really believed that their cats could come back to life nine times. The number 9 was sacred, apparently because 3 was sacred, and there were three 3's in 9. The number 3 became sacred so long ago that no one can say exactly why people thought it had special meaning.

There were a great many other ancient superstitions about numbers. Seven was considered lucky by the Hebrews, Babylonians, Assyrians, Aztec Indians and others. The seventh son of a seventh son was supposed to have supernatural powers.

The Japanese have some numbers that mean good luck and wealth, and others that mean business failure or death. This makes it very difficult for the telephone company, because there are certain numbers that no Japanese wants to have. Even if he isn't superstitious, himself, his friends or customers may be. On the other hand, people are willing to pay a high price for a lucky number. The unlucky ones are often given to foreigners who do not have the same prejudices.

Colours, as well as numbers, have often been considered lucky or unlucky. Among Navaho Indians, red is bad and blue is good, but certain Armenian tribes had a fierce hatred of blue. Green was a sacred colour among some Moslems. Purple has long been the colour of kings in certain countries. To the ancient Greeks, black was the colour of death. This idea spread and had a strong effect on much of Europe. Now, in many places, black clothes are worn as a sign of mourning for the dead. In China, however, white was the colour for mourning.

WHY IS 13 SUPPOSED TO BE AN UNLUCKY NUMBER?

LONG AGO, people in certain places counted by twelves instead of by tens, as most of us do today. And twelve really was a convenient number. It was made up of six 2's; or four 3's, or three 4's, or two 6's. Because twelve was so handy, people often formed themselves into groups of twelve. Then they added one more person to be leader. In ancient Europe, certain religious services were conducted by a priest with twelve helpers.

This combination of twelve and one — which, of course, made thirteen — appeared in many forms that were supposed to have magic meaning and to bring good luck. But magic can work evil as well as good. In parts of Europe, the priestess was finally thought to be a witch with twelve other witches helping her. In Scandinavia, according to a viking legend, a god named Loki once came to dinner with twelve other gods, one of whom was blind. Cruel Loki persuaded the blind god to kill Baldur, the son of a goddess. Because this terrible thing happened when there

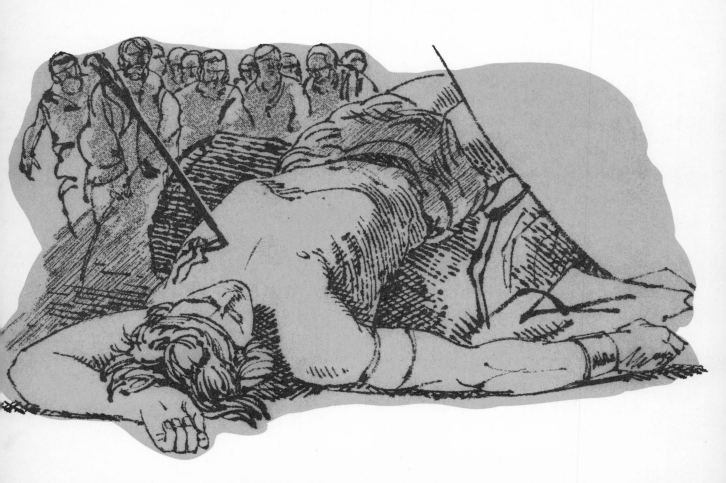

were thirteen together at dinner, pagans decided it was better to avoid having thirteen at one table, or even at one gathering. Christians remembered the story of a different dinner that made them dread the number thirteen. At the Last Supper, Jesus sat at the table with his twelve disciples, one of whom betrayed him.

Perhaps because of stories like these, the number thirteen came to be regarded as unlucky for any kind of use. Today, even in a great modern city such as New York, there are some skyscrapers in which the thirteenth floor is not labelled 13. It is called 12A or even 14. The owners of the buildings say they have found it difficult to rent rooms on the thirteenth floor. To many people, 13 is still connected with misfortune.

According to one old belief, there is a way to avoid bad luck when thirteen people find themselves seated together. If all thirteen should join hands and stand up, no harm will come to any of them!

WHY IS FRIDAY THE 13TH SUPPOSED TO BE UNLUCKY?

FRIDAY WAS a sacred day among various ancient tribes. It was a day for religious ceremonies, and people felt that the gods would be displeased if human beings did any work on that day. This belief grew and changed. If it was bad luck to work on Friday, it might be bad luck to do anything at all on Friday. Gradually, Friday itself became linked with bad luck.

People also had the notion that 13 was an unlucky number. Clearly, if the number and the day came together, Friday the 13th must be very unlucky, indeed.

WHY DO PEOPLE SAY, "KNOCK ON WOOD"?

IN MANY parts of the world there was once a belief that gods lived in trees, and so wood was sacred. If a person wanted help from a tree god, he reached out and touched wood. The custom continued long after people gave up that particular religious belief. Without knowing why they did it, they kept on touching or knocking on wood when they wanted to keep something bad from happening.

The Etruscan people had this kind of mirror more than two thousand years ago.

WILL YOU HAVE 7 YEARS OF BAD LUCK IF YOU BREAK A MIRROR?

WHEN A man first looked into a mirror made of polished stone or metal, he thought he was seeing a twin self. This other self seemed like his soul, and the mirror seemed to hold it. Of course, any object that held a thing as valuable as a man's soul had to be protected.

The Etruscan people, who lived in Italy before the Romans, had this belief, and the Romans borrowed it. The Romans also believed that every living thing began a new life every seven years. If it was injured, it would become whole again only after seven years had passed. So if a mirror was damaged, the soul it contained was also harmed and would not be whole again for seven years.

This problem wasn't very serious, because mirrors of polished metal or stone did not break easily. But in the fourteenth century, Italian glass-makers invented glass mirrors, which were quite fragile. At that time the old Roman superstition still lived on, and people remembered it when they got the new mirrors made of glass. They began to say that to break one would bring seven years of bad luck. Today, almost nobody who repeats this saying knows that the superstition grew out of an attempt to explain why light reflected from a shiny surface can give a man an image of himself.

The first known rear-view mirror was put up in a hallway in the palace where the Roman emperor Domitian took walks. He was afraid his enemies might steal up behind him and stab him in the back.

WHY DO PEOPLE SAY, "KEEP YOUR FINGERS CROSSED"?

Long ago, when two people wanted the same thing to happen, one of them would hold out an index finger and the other would lay his index finger against it, making a cross. The cross was a symbol which they thought would bring good luck, and among Christians it also stood for unity.

In time, the belief in crossed fingers gradually changed. It was thought that one person alone could magically make a wish come true if he crossed his middle finger over his index finger. Finally, it was enough just to say, "I'll keep my fingers crossed," which simply meant, "I wish that nothing may happen to spoil my hopes."

WHY IS A FOUR-LEAF CLOVER SUPPOSED TO BE LUCKY?

According to one story, Eve took a four-leaf clover with her when she was driven out of the Garden of Eden, which was also called Paradise. Ever afterward, anyone who had a clover with four leaves had a little bit of Paradise. Obviously, such a person was lucky.

In Ireland, more than two thousand years ago, clover was sacred to a group of people called druids. A druid was a combination of teacher, priest and magician. A four-leaf clover forms a cross, and the druids thought a cross was a sign of luck. So, in Ireland, it was easy to attach special meaning to a plant shaped like a cross.

Farmers have often thought it lucky to have a patch of clover growing in a field, and this belief could have been based on observation. Clover is one of a small group of plants that can absorb nitrogen from the air and turn it into a substance that fertilizes the soil and helps other plants to grow well.

WHEN DID MAN DISCOVER CURES FOR SICKNESS?

FOR MANY thousands of years people tried to cure diseases by magic. They held ceremonies to drive away sickness or to prevent it, and they prescribed medicines. Some of the ancient medicines were made of such ingredients as powdered bone, feathers, hair and snake meat. Nobody knows all of the reasons for these concoctions, but patients believed in them.

Other medicines were made from plants, and many of them really did help. For example, a substance that comes from the coca plant can stop pain. Indians in South America discovered this and doctors today still use a pain-killing coca-leaf drug called cocaine. Doctors also prescribe ancient plant remedies for heart trouble, stomach-ache and various other complaints.

Most of man's worst diseases could not be cured by old-time medicines. Still, doctors kept trying to find remedies. They became very skillful at recognizing illnesses. They learned what each one was likely to do to a patient, and this knowledge became very important in Babylon, where laws about the practice of medicine were very strict. Suppose a Babylonian doctor tried to cure a man's eye and failed. The doctor's own eye would be put out.

In Greece, where athletic activity was considered very important, doctors learned how to set broken bones and treat strained muscles. The Greeks had a special god of medicine named Aesculapius, and priests in his temples took part in healing ceremonies. People who wanted to be cured stayed in special buildings which became the first big hospitals. When the old Greek religion disappeared, the hospitals were abandoned, too.

Hundreds of years went by. A few doctors kept on being interested in the human body and how it worked, but they did very little investigating. Some of them did examine the heart, liver and other organs of dead animals, but they came to very strange conclusions. One said that the heart was a kind of furnace for heating the blood. We still use an expression that reflects this belief when we say that a person has "a warm heart." "Kind-hearted" dates back to the Egyptian doctors who thought the heart controlled man's conscience and sense of duty.

Many of these old beliefs lasted until a scientific-minded English doctor began to question them. He made experiments — something that most doctors thought was unnecessary. In 1628 he wrote a book that explained how the heart pumps the blood throughout the body. For a long while afterward everyone laughed at him.

Meantime, Turks, Africans and Chinese had made a wonderful discovery about smallpox: you weren't so likely to die from it if you were given a mild case of the disease on purpose. Most doctors in England scoffed at this idea when they first heard it. But a few years later, in 1721, some men in Massachusetts tried it and lived through an epidemic. By the end of that century, an Englishman discovered vaccination, which kept most people from getting as much as a mild form of smallpox. Now, for the first time in history, doctors could control a disease, although they had not the slightest idea why vaccination succeeded.

Finally, in the nineteenth century, with the help of microscopes, doctors and chemists worked out the germ theory of disease. So it was only about a hundred years ago that the real science of medicine could begin.

An African healer. In his medicine kit are pieces of bone covered with markings. He tosses the bones into the air, and when they land, he looks at the sides that show. The markings, he believes, tell him the cause of a sick person's disease. Games of dice probably started out as a similar device used by healers long ago.

WHEN DID SCIENCE BEGIN?

WHEN PEOPLE were very new on earth, life must have been rather monotonous. They had to spend much of their time looking for food, wandering about over a large area, and one group seldom met another. Each little band knew only its own area. With no way to compare animals and plants and human beings from other places, people had few surprises to start them wondering. But they must have wondered a little. Stone Age men and women and children may have asked, "What is the wind trying to say?" Or, "Why did that rock bump me in the toe?"

By asking questions and trying to figure out answers, people got many good ideas. But they also got notions that didn't quite fit the facts. Some people, for example, decided that the wind was alive, though invisible, and that a rock, too, could have a life of its own. Before they could find answers that really explained nature, they had to find the right questions to ask.

Questions had to begin before there could be any science. But that wasn't all. People had to observe things carefully and wonder how one set of observations fitted in with another. For example, the seasons came and went regularly; the stars changed position in the sky. Could the stars, by their positions, tell when the rainy season was about to begin? They could. This kind of thinking gave astronomy — the first science — its start at least five thousand years ago.

It was not always easy for an observer to get the right answer. For example, after men discovered that a magnet attracted iron, European sailors concluded that there were magnetic islands in the Indian Ocean. They reasoned this way: European ships, which had iron nails in their construction, seemed to be drawn irresistibly toward the islands. Ships that had been built without iron nails seemed not to be drawn to the islands. Since there was no important difference between the two kinds of ships, except for the nails, the sailors could think of only one explanation: magnetism in the islands must be pulling on the iron in their ships.

The real explanation was quite different. Strong ocean currents moved

Before the modern science of chemistry developed, men known as alchemists did experiments with metals, acids and other substances. The alchemists hoped to make gold from cheaper metals, and they kept at it for more than 1,500 years. Gradually they compiled a great deal of practical knowledge about chemicals. By the seventeenth century, this knowledge had become useful to industries, such as soap-manufacture and cloth-dyeing. The alchemists gave up their old dream of making gold, and they became practical experimenters. Alchemy probably started in China and moved from there to India, Egypt and Europe.

all vessels toward the islands, but the native boatmen knew about the currents and avoided them. It was just coincidence that their vessels happened to be put together without iron nails.

What would a scientist have done in order to hunt for the true answer? He would have made tests, of course. Watching, wondering, putting facts together and then testing — these are some of the main tools of science. But it was easier to use them on some things than on others. Men could explain a magnifying glass long before they had any idea how eyes worked. There had been astronomers for thousands of years before chemists began to develop their own science in the seventeenth century. *Science* is an old word that comes from the Latin for *knowledge,* yet the word *scientist* was invented only in the year 1840.

WAS THERE A REAL KING ARTHUR?

About A.D. 500, fierce warriors from northern Europe invaded Britain. Some belonged to a tribe called Angles and some were Saxons. Between them they conquered the native Britons. At that time there seems to have been a chief among the Britons whose name was Arthur. That is as much as we know about "King" Arthur. However, a great many stories have been told about him. The oldest of these stories are like the tales of conquered people in many places. They tell of a saviour who can do miraculous deeds and who will one day free the oppressed. Some of the tales seem to have been mixed with the legends of Wales.

The belief in magic was strong at that time, and real events were easily confused with sorcery and witchcraft. That probably explains why there were supposed to be thirteen at King Arthur's Round Table — the King, himself, and his twelve knights. Ancient witchcraft ceremonies were held by both men and women who met in groups of thirteen called *covens*. (There are still people in England today who call themselves witches and who belong to covens.)

The legends about King Arthur kept growing for hundreds of years. Stories of the Crusades were added to the original tales. Finally, a thousand years after Arthur actually lived, a man named Sir Thomas Malory combined many of the legends about him into a book. Malory was in prison at the time. He had been arrested for various kinds of rebellious activity, and he wrote to pass the time while he was serving his sentence.

WAS THERE A REAL GENGHIS KHAN?

A boy named Temujin was born near Lake Baikal in Siberia about 1162. His people were Mongols, and he belonged to a group whose name, translated into English, meant *Golden*. They lived in a large tent made of felt which they took down and moved easily whenever their bands of horses needed new pasture. Milk from the horses was nourishing food, and Temujin grew to be a strong, fierce, skilled rider. He became a chief among his own people. Then he united many groups of nomads and led them all in an invasion of China.

By the time Temujin was forty-four years old, he was called the Greatest of all Rulers, which in his language was Chingis or Jenghis or Genghis Khan. After he had subdued China, he moved westward and conquered Central Asia and much of Russia. His warrior people came to be called the *Golden Horde*. *Horde* is based on a word that among some wandering tribes meant *camp* or *those who camp together*.

Genghis Khan died in 1227, but his family and descendants ruled the land between China and Russia for about three hundred years. Even after they were driven back into Mongolia, many Mongols went on honouring his memory. They kept his bones (or perhaps his ashes) in a silver chest sealed shut with locks of gold. Since the Mongols were nomads, the chest travelled with them and had its own tent. Seven hundred years after Genghis Khan's death, the tent was still being carried about on a cart drawn by white camels.

WHO WERE THE MOGULS?

DESCENDANTS of the Mongol Genghis Khan were called Moguls in India, where they began to rule in 1526. The Mogul Empire grew and united most of India. Then it began to lose influence until, in 1857, it was overthrown by a British army. Twenty years later, in 1877, Britain's Queen Victoria received the title, "Empress of India."

69

WHEN DID CARD GAMES START?

CHINESE PEOPLE have often said that one of their emperors invented playing cards for the amusement of his wives. The exact year was supposed to have been 1120. Most historians believe that card games are even older than that. At any rate, the idea started in Asia and spread to Europe.

Some of the early cards were beautifully painted by hand, and only a few people had them. When printing was invented, cards became cheaper and more people played games with them. The pictures on cards varied from one country to another, but the designs and figures generally had some meaning. The 52-card packs used in America and in much of Europe today still have symbols that are several hundred years old. Hearts stand for the clergy, diamonds for merchants, clubs for peasants, and spades for soldiers. (*Spade* comes from the Spanish word *espada,* meaning *sword.*)

During the American and French Revolutions, some people were so strongly opposed to royalty that they tried to get rid of the kings and queens in card decks. But those who liked the old games went right on playing them, and after a while, almost everyone forgot the whole thing. Since cards are often used in gambling, efforts have been made in the past to abolish all card-playing.

Fortunetelling by means of cards came to Europe in the fourteenth century. At that time, bands of wandering people began to appear in country after country. They were gifted musicians, dark-haired and handsome, and the songs they sang in their strange language were wild and sad. They had a talent for acting, too. Some merrily pretended to be noblemen from Egypt. The kings of France, Spain and Scotland provided lavish entertainment for them. Where these people really came from no one knew, and it remained a secret for nearly five hundred years. In their own language, their name was *Rom,* which means simply *man.* In English, they were called Gypsies.

Gypsy men were very good at metalworking and training horses. The women told fortunes with decks of what are called tarot cards. For a while, their skills and music made them welcome as they wandered about over

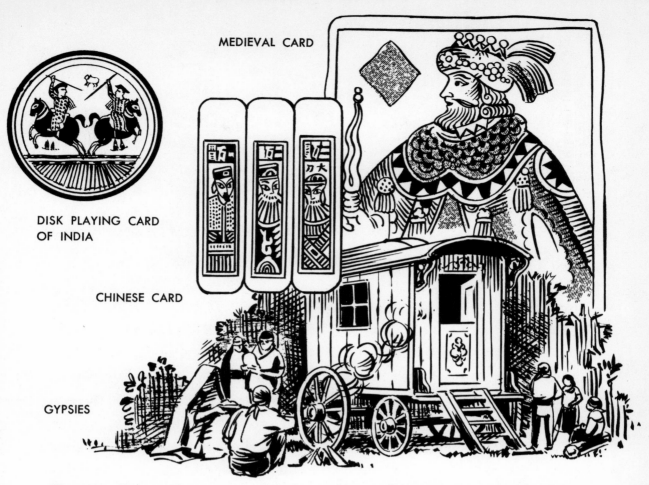

DISK PLAYING CARD
OF INDIA

MEDIEVAL CARD

CHINESE CARD

GYPSIES

Europe. Later, they were called witches and sorcerers, and they were persecuted. But through all their sufferings they kept their language, their music and their ancient customs.

During World War II, the Nazis killed half a million Gypsies. Many others have survived, but they find it increasingly difficult to lead a wandering life in the modern world. Only a few Gypsies can read or write. In some places, governments have tried to help them settle down and find jobs. Some countries have experimented with classrooms built on trucks, so that schools can travel along with the children.

Although the problem of educating Gypsies hasn't been solved, the mystery of their homeland has been. A few years ago, a group of scientists traced the Gypsy language back to a part of India on the edge of the Himalaya Mountains. There, they are quite sure, the ancestors of the Gypsies once lived in tents and ruled over an empire. Then Mongols from the north invaded their land. Those who wanted to remain free began the wanderings that have not ended to this day.

WHO INVENTED CHESS?

MANY EXPERTS think chess was played originally in India. From there it travelled westward, and players in various countries made changes in the game. Today's rules were adopted in Europe sometime about A.D. 1550.

The pieces used in chess have names that tell something about European life in the sixteenth century and before. There are kings, queens, bishops and knights. Most of the pieces are pawns. That word comes from the old French word for *foot soldier*. The game itself is a mock battle of the kind that kings and churchmen, too, carried on in real life centuries ago.

One chess piece is known by two names, castle or rook. There were certainly castles all over Europe, but the word *rook* gives a clue to the earlier history of the game. It comes from another word, *roc,* which in the ancient Persian language meant a mythical bird that was so large it could carry off an elephant. How it got mixed up with chess is not clear.

A player says "Checkmate!" when he moves a piece in such a way that the other player cannot make a move without losing his king. This ends the game. The word *checkmate* was a mispronunciation of an Arabian phrase. It came from *al-shah-mat,* meaning *the king is dead. Checkers* comes from the same source, and the game itself resembles chess in simplified form. No one knows just where it started.

Some historians think that chess and checkers did not start out as games. Instead, they were used by fortunetellers who believed that the position of the pieces on the board could show what would happen in the future. Dice probably started in the same way.

72

WHEN DID THE OLYMPIC GAMES START?

THE FIRST recorded Olympic Games were part of a religious ceremony and took place in Greece in 776 B.C. After that, the games were held every four years for more than a thousand years. During much of that time, warring Greek armies stopped their fighting when the sacred Olympics took place, and athletes from both sides could enter the competitions.

In 1894, a French educator, Baron Pierre de Coubertin, began to urge that the Olympics be revived. He believed they would increase international friendship and understanding. The Olympic Games have been held since 1896, usually every four years, but in 1916, 1940 and 1944 they were cancelled because of war.

In recent years, more than ninety nations have sent teams to the games. Champions come from many countries and many racial groups. An Ethiopian won the marathon in 1960 and 1964. The most populous country in the world, the People's Republic of China, has not yet entered teams in the Olympics, but in 1960, a Chinese from the island of Formosa nearly won first place in the hardest event of all, the decathlon. Contestants in the decathlon must compete against each other in ten different events. The champion in 1960 was Rafer Johnson, an American Negro. Willi Holdorf, a German, won the 1964 championship.

From time to time, new contests have been added. The Winter Olympics began in 1924, and for some reason, there are even Olympic contests in architecture and sculpture.

We know what early Olympic runners looked like, because drawings of them were made into decorations on Greek pottery.

WERE ATHLETES BETTER IN THE PAST?

SOME ATHLETES of the past may have been better than any in the same sport today. But in most sports, where it is possible to make real comparisons, the best athletes now surpass the top competitors of the past. In 1864, the world's record for the mile run was 4 minutes, 56 seconds. In 1969, it was 3 minutes, 51.1 seconds.

Why?

For one thing, many athletes are now trained scientifically. Experts prepare the right food for them. Doctors make careful studies and work out schemes for overcoming exhaustion. The first man to run a mile in less than four minutes was a medical student who studied carefully what his body could be made to do. Mathematicians help high jumpers learn just how far they should run, and when and how they should jump in order to lift their bodies as high in the air as possible. Athletes study movies of themselves and of the champions. The films disclose the mistakes to avoid, as well as the good things to imitate.

Every year there are more people in the world, which means that there are more boys and girls with athletic ability. The search for these young people is more efficient than it used to be. Coaches and scouts watch for boys and girls who look as if they might develop into champions. In the United States and the Soviet Union — the countries that have the best track and field teams — there are local contests from which winners go on to regional, then to national meets.

Athletic contests today are usually open to everyone. In the past, in various countries, many sports were closed to the children of workingmen. Until 1947, no Negroes in the United States were allowed to play major-league baseball, and professional tennis was also closed to those whose skins were not white. But when the games were made more democratic, people of different races quickly showed their abilities. Althea Gibson won both the United States and British women's tennis singles championships in 1957. In 1965, Arthur Ashe, a Negro, was acclaimed one of the best tennis players in the world. In the 1964 Olympics, 18 of the 67 members of the United States men's track and field team were Negroes, as were 15 of the 20 members of the United States women's team.

A look at the pictures will show one reason why women can now play tennis better and swim faster than in the old days.

WHEN WAS THE FIRST FOOTBALL GAME PLAYED?

ANCIENT AZTECS, Eskimos, Chinese and South Sea Islanders all played some kind of game in which a ball was kicked about. So did Greeks, Romans and European tribesmen called Teutons and Celts. Such games were also very popular in England during the Middle Ages. Men and boys often played in the streets. Once, when the winter was cold enough, there was even a football game on the ice on the River Thames.

A writer in the time of Queen Elizabeth I said, "The players kick each other's shins without the least ceremony." In the rough-and-tumble of the game, injuries were frequent, but the sport remained popular century after century. In 1863, many British football clubs banded together to form an association, and thereafter the type of game they played was called association football. Americans called it soccer, a word that comes from the *soc* in *association*. Soccer is now played in many parts of the world and is included in the Olympic Games, where it is simply called football. There are eleven players on a team, and it is a kicking game. Players are not allowed to carry the ball.

One day in 1823, a boy at Rugby public school broke the no-carrying rule. He picked up the ball and ran with it. After getting over their astonishment, other players on the field decided that maybe this rule-breaking boy had a good idea. From that day a new kind of football began to develop. It was Rugby, named after the school where it had been invented. With fifteen men on each side, the game is still popular in Britain and several countries of the British Commonwealth. Many French athletes play it, and there are a number of Rugby teams in the United States.

American football teams played soccer until 1874. That year Harvard's team played a two-game series against the Rugby team of McGill University of Montreal, Canada. One game was to be played according to soccer rules, the other according to the rules of Rugby. The Harvard players liked Rugby so much that they kept on playing it after they got back home. The game spread far and wide, but it began to change. Teams in the United States had eleven players, as in soccer, instead of the fifteen on a regular Rugby team. In 1905, President Theodore Roosevelt took an interest in the game, and with his encouragement the rules were again changed. Players could now throw the ball forward as well as carry it. From then on, the forward pass became part of the United States variety of football.

At least ten different forms of football are played in the world today.

WHY IS A FOOTBALL SHAPED LIKE AN EGG?

In England, footballs were first made by putting a leather covering over an animal bladder that was shaped somewhat like an egg. After manufacturers began to make bladders of rubber, they still kept the old shape for the balls used in the game called Rugby. The ball, with its egglike shape, was easy to carry and nobody wanted to change it.

But the invention of rubber bladders also made it possible for balls to be perfectly spherical. These were easier to control in the all-kicking game of soccer — and so round balls came into use in soccer.

After Rugby became popular in the United States, some experimenter made a rubber bladder that was a little more slender than the regular animal bladder. The result was a ball that could be carried very easily. It could also be kicked through the air with more control and thrown with great accuracy. The fact that this new ball could be thrown so well was one reason why the forward pass could be introduced into the American kind of football.

WHEN DID BASEBALL BEGIN?

FOR CENTURIES, English children played a certain game with a ball and a bat. If the batter hit the ball, he then tried to run around some bases. Because of this running around, the game was called rounders. One way to put out a runner was to throw the ball at him and hit him before he got back to the place from which he started.

When English people began to settle in America, they brought along their games, including rounders. About 1840, some unknown American rounders player thought of a new way of putting out a runner. Instead of hitting the runner with a thrown ball, why not simply require an opposing player to hold the ball in his hand and touch or tag a runner with it? Players tried out this idea and liked it. The new rule became popular and spread.

The old rounders ball was soft. It could hit a runner without injuring him. Now the ball could be hard, since it was no longer thrown at a runner. A batter could knock a hard ball much farther than he could a soft ball, and this brought about a great change in the nature of the game. With the introduction of the hard ball, baseball began.

For a long time, people liked to say that Abner Doubleday of Cooperstown, New York, invented baseball, and there is, in fact, a big baseball museum at Cooperstown. However, there is little evidence that Doubleday had anything to do with inventing the game. Perhaps the story got started at a time when Americans, with a kind of national pride, liked to think they had invented everything that was typically American. Actually, players in the New World borrowed much of the idea for baseball from the Old World, just as people everywhere have always borrowed from each other.

WHEN DID BASKETBALL BEGIN?

IN 1891, eighteen boys in a class in Springfield, Massachusetts, were bored with the physical exercises they had to take. At that same time, a young Canadian named James Naismith, an instructor at the Young Men's Christian Association Training School in Springfield, decided there was no good reason why exercise shouldn't be fun. Why not make up a new game? By December he had worked out the idea: Each of two teams would try to score by tossing a ball into a basket. In January, 1892, he divided the class of eighteen boys into two teams of nine each, and they played the first basketball game in history. High on the wall at each end of the Y.M.C.A. gymnasium was an actual basket — a peach basket. In 1897, the number of players was reduced to five on each team, and that is the number today.

Basketball has more spectators than any other game in the United States, and it is also very popular in many other countries. Since 1936, it has been one of the sports in the Olympic Games.

Before Columbus discovered America, a game something like basketball was played by the Maya Indians. The players tried to bounce a rubber ball through a stone hoop high on the wall of the ball court. Almost four hundred years after Columbus, this ancient Indian game was discussed in a report made by an archeologist in Massachusetts at just about the time modern basketball was invented. Question: Did the inventor of basketball get his idea from the Maya Indians?

WHO INVENTED SHAVING?

SOME EXPERTS believe that shaving was a very ancient religious ceremony. They are not sure whether it began in Egypt or Sumer. Wherever it began, the custom spread and most people forgot its religious meanings. Three thousand years ago, men in Denmark shaped bronze into razors. A razor,

BEDS were invented in Asia Minor, improved in Egypt, made more comfortable in Europe. The Greeks had SHOWER BATHS.

CORN FLAKES are made from corn, first grown by American Indians. MILK, of course, comes from cows; cows were first milked in Asia Minor. ORANGES were first grown in Indo-China, imported to Spain, and carried by Spaniards to the Americas.

Stone Age people invented ROPE.

UMBRELLAS were invented in southeast Asia.

made of copper about five thousand years ago, was found in Egypt.

As with razors, almost everything we use and eat and wear has a long history. People have constantly borrowed the ideas and materials of other people, and we are fortunate to have thousands of years of borrowing behind us. As a result, our lives arc filled with wonderful inventions that have come from many lands and earlier times.

BICYCLES were invented by a German, improved by an Englishman.

WRITING was invented in Sumer; PAPER, in China; modern PRINTING was developed in Germany.

PYJAMAS came from India; COTTON for the cloth probably came from Arabia.

The LIGHT BULB was invented by an American, Thomas A. Edison.

WHEN WERE THE MIDDLE AGES?

THERE ARE no exact dates for the Middle Ages, but many historians say that they began about A.D. 300 and lasted for at least a thousand years. The period is called the Middle Ages because it comes in the middle, between ancient times and modern times.

WHAT WERE THE DARK AGES?

THE FIRST few hundred years of the Middle Ages in Western Europe have sometimes been called the Dark Ages. Most historians now merely talk about the Early Middle Ages. At that time the ancient empire of the Romans was fading away. Its armies no longer repaired roads or even used them. There was very little travel, business or trade. People moved out of the cities and towns and lived on the land in order to get food. Finally, Western Europe was taken over by tribes of people who had once been conquered by the Romans.

Slowly, however, these tribes, with their own rulers, began to cut down forests and make good new farms. They built villages. They set up mills to grind flour and to saw wood and manufacture iron. Trade started again. Although life was still very hard for almost everybody, by the tenth century it was not so lonely and isolated as before.

It was only the western part of the old Roman Empire that broke apart so completely. In Eastern Europe and North Africa and Asia, trade and business did not die when the Empire ended. The cities and towns did not shrivel up. They remained lively places where artists, writers and scholars worked and taught.

In the Far East during this time the Chinese made important inventions. One was the compass. At first, a compass was probably a fortune-telling device, made from a piece of magnetic iron ore. This rock, sometimes called lodestone, was carved into the shape of a dipper with a rounded bowl, possibly to imitate the Dipper in the sky, which pointed toward the North Star. In addition to the lodestone, the fortuneteller had a board with magical symbols around the edge. When he tossed the dipper onto the board, it would balance on its rounded bowl, swing this way and that, and finally come to rest pointing north and south. After looking at the symbols toward which the lodestone pointed, the fortuneteller would explain what they stood for — perhaps good luck or bad, sickness or health.

By the sixth century, the Chinese had discovered that they could magnetize iron by rubbing it with lodestone. Before long, someone thought of balancing a magnetized iron needle in the centre of a card that showed directions. This, of course, was a compass. From China it was taken to Europe, where sailors knew about it by the eleventh century. Probably Leif Ericson had one of the wonderful north-pointing needles to guide him on his voyage to North America.

The compass made it possible for men to explore more and more of the world. With exploration came increased trade and knowledge, and the beginning of modern times.

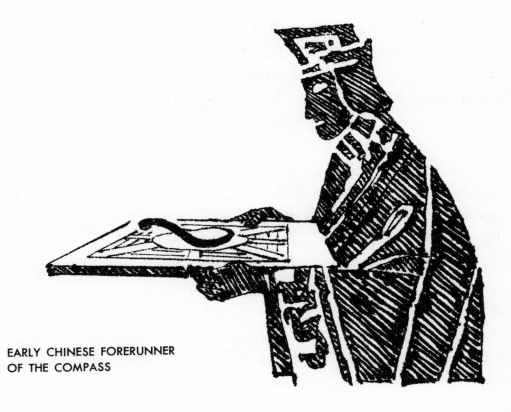

EARLY CHINESE FORERUNNER
OF THE COMPASS

WHO WAS WILLIAM THE CONQUEROR?

SCANDINAVIAN TRIBESMEN, called vikings or Norsemen, raided and conquered many lands in the ninth and tenth centuries. Some of them settled in England, where they became rulers of the country and learned to speak the language of the people around them. Other Norsemen made their homes in France, where they adopted the French language. These French Norsemen were called Normans, a shortened form of the same word.

In 1066 the King of England died, and there began among the warlike Norsemen a great scramble for power. One army came from Norway, bent on winning the English throne for its leader. While the English were defeating it, an army of Normans came from France. Near Hastings, in the county of Sussex, these French invaders outwitted the English by pretending to flee. When the English started in disorderly pursuit, the Normans turned and cut them to pieces.

The Norman duke who devised this trick went on to London and had himself crowned king. His name was William, and he has become known as William the Conqueror. His father had been a warrior in the

Norse tradition. His mother was a humble French girl whom his father never married.

William was a huge man, fierce and full of energy, and he understood very well how to organize a government based on force. He took big estates away from some of the English lords, then gave the land to nobles from France, making them rich and powerful. These Norman nobles were the ancestors of many of the aristocratic families in England today.

The new Norman rulers brought with them knowledge and skills that their armies had gained from other people they had conquered. They also brought along the French language. Many of their words became established alongside old English words. For example, the conquering Normans ate *beef, mutton* and *veal*, while the peasants who supplied the meat continued to use the old words *ox, sheep* and *calf*. Because William the Conqueror turned French knights into noblemen, English now has words like *castle, countess* and *court*. The warlike Normans gave Englishmen *prison* and *grief*, too; on the other hand, their invasion also brought the word *peace*.

HOW DID COUNTRIES GET STARTED?

SOMETIMES a country got started when a city enlarged its territory by conquering other cities. Sometimes groups of people joined each other and willingly chose one leader for all. Countries have also been formed when separate groups joined to defend themselves against a powerful wandering tribe. When many areas were brought together under the control of one king or emperor, an empire was formed.

In ancient times around the Mediterranean Sea, one city after another would grow strong, build an empire, and then lose it. The Roman Empire was the last big one. After it fell apart, in the fifth century, there were no large countries or states in western Europe for several centuries. Instead, hundreds of small areas called principalities had local rulers. But gradually, in order to make trade or defense easier, some of these principalities joined together of their own free will. Others were united by conquerors. Separate European countries developed, but their borders kept changing because rulers fought for control of territory.

Beginning in the fifteenth century, some of these rather small countries of Europe began to build large empires. Their armies seized lands in distant parts of the world and turned them into colonies. Portugal, France, Holland, Spain and Britain all had empires in the Americas, Asia and Africa.

Then a new trend started. Some conquered countries won freedom. In North America, thirteen British colonies rebelled in 1776 and became the United States. About fifty years later Spain's South American colonies began to rebel. So did Portugal's. After the Second World War, old empires broke up even more quickly. Helped in some ways by the United Nations, more than fifty former colonies became independent countries. The map shows those which gained independence between 1943 and 1966.

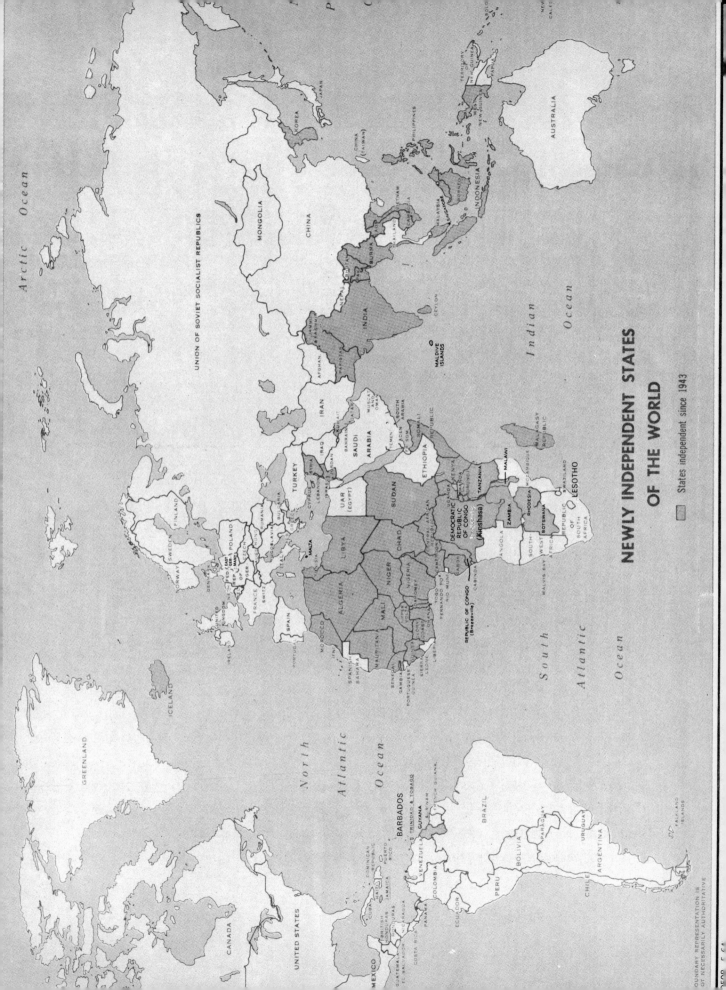

NEWLY INDEPENDENT STATES
OF THE WORLD

☐ States independent since 1943

TOTEM POLE   ROMAN STANDARD   EGYPTIAN STANDARD

WHEN WERE FLAGS FIRST MADE?

THE HISTORY of flags started in prehistoric times, long before there was anything we call a flag. In those days men were hunters, and they felt very close to the whole animal world. They drew pictures of animals and carved them in wood or stone. Perhaps some people thought that they got magic help from one particular creature. They may even have believed that a distant ancestor of theirs was a bear or a coyote or an eagle. At any rate, groups of people who were relatives (they are called clans) often adopted the name of an animal or bird or fish, and it then became a clan symbol. The word for this clan symbol, in the language of one American Indian tribe, was *totem*. Now all such symbols are called totems.

Carvings of totems were sometimes placed over doors or on poles in front of houses. Warriors carried their totems into battle. The animal or bird was often painted on their shields, or its image might be carried on a long stick called a standard. This custom proved useful. When soldiers were scattered during a fight, they could rejoin their fellows by looking for the standard that belonged to their leader.

Standards were used more as armies grew bigger. In Egypt the totem of the ruler — the Pharaoh — was a falcon, and the Pharaoh had feathers attached to a pole held high above his warriors. Assyrian soldiers rallied around a disc that was held aloft. On it was painted a bull or two bulls tied together by their tails. Greek armies followed similar totems — an owl for the city of Athens, a winged horse for Corinth, a bull for Boeotia. One fast-moving army even had a slow-moving tortoise on its standard.

Later, Roman armies followed the same custom of carrying animal totems. There were five of these in service for a long time. Then a Roman leader took away four of them and left only an eagle. The eagle, however, did not remain the only symbol. Soldiers adopted others. Some were put on pieces of cloth which hung suspended along the top edges.

A different kind of flag flew over battles in Persia in 80 B.C. At that time the Persians revolted against a particularly despotic ruler, and their leader was a blacksmith. His work-apron was raised as a standard above the fighting.

In 1100 B.C., Chinese armies had begun to use flags made just as flags are made today — attached by a side edge. From China this idea moved westward. Finally it was adopted by Moslem armies in the seventh or eighth century. Christian Crusaders later fought with the Moslems. The flags caught the Crusaders' fancy, and soon this new kind of emblem became fashionable in Europe.

A war fought to make people change their ideas is called a crusade. Wars of that sort were carried on by Moslems in Africa and Asia in the seventh and eighth centuries. Then Christians from Western Europe set forth on seven crusades against the Moslems, beginning in the eleventh century. After these crusades, the Christian area of the world was smaller than before. On the other hand, people in Western Europe learned from the Moslems about new foods, new ways to build castles and churches — and the idea of orange blossoms for the bride at a wedding.

IS A COAT OF ARMS THE SAME AS A FLAG?

IN THE MIDDLE AGES, during the Crusades, it became fashionable for knights to have a coat of arms. Originally, these were designs that knights put on cloth coats worn over their armour. (The cloth helped to keep sunlight from making the metal armour too hot.) Later, the designs themselves got the name *coat of arms*. Another name for them was *armorial bearings*.

Like a clan totem, the design in a coat of arms told some kind of story. It might include birds and flowers, lions, dragons or other symbols for things that were important in a man's life. When a father died, his children and their descendants inherited the family coat of arms.

At the time of the First Crusade, the Pope ordered all crusaders to wear coats bearing the sign of the cross. Around the cross a man could add other designs, if he liked. The cross was a badge indicating that the wearer was a Christian. Other Christians were supposed to give him help when he travelled toward the Near East to fight Moslems.

Designs on a coat had another use. Without them, men in armour all looked very much alike, and there was no way to tell one from another if their helmets were closed. In battle it was a good idea to know which knights were your friends and which ones were your foes. Bright coats of arms helped solve the problem. This may have been one reason why the custom of wearing the emblems became so popular.

The nobility liked the idea of coats of arms. They had the designs

JERUSALEM

GERMANY

RUSSIA

FRISIA

carved into decorations above stone gates, painted on dishes, embroidered on banners and woven into cloth. After a while, men known as heralds began to specialize in learning everything there was to know about such symbols. They called their studies heraldry, and they could find out a great deal about a man's ancestors just by looking at his coat of arms.

Heralds invented a special vocabulary. For example, the word for red was *gules*. Gold and silver were *metal*. It was considered improper to design a new coat of arms with metal touching metal. In other words, gold and silver should never be placed next to each other. European flags still follow this rule — except for one. Gold touches silver in the flag of Vatican City, where the Roman Catholic Pope lives and works.

After men stopped wearing armour, coats of arms were no longer so useful in battle, but they still remained popular among the nobility and among people who wanted to be nobles. Heralds kept on with their work, and there are heralds today in England. They have charge of royal ceremonies, and they design new coats of arms and new flags for special purposes.

A coat of arms was once a symbol used only by a family. Later, a city or a country might have one. It is not the same as a national flag, but many national flags developed out of coats of arms.

By the middle of the fourteenth century, each of Europe's many tiny countries seems to have adopted its own flag or symbol. Pictures of them appeared in a book written by a Spanish priest.

Here are some of the illustrations from that first book about flags.

GRANADA

JAVA

TOULOUSE

FRANCE

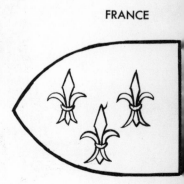

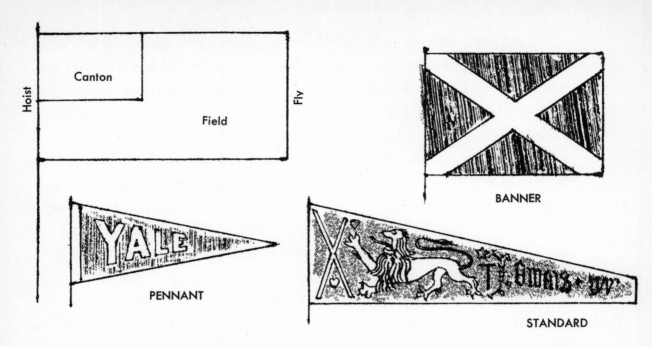

IS A FLAG THE SAME AS A BANNER OR A PENNANT?

BANNERS, pennants, ensigns, standards and colours are all flags. There are distinctions between them, and the words sometimes mean different things in different countries. The pictures show a few of the many types.

A national flag can be called a banner. Clubs, unions and special groups of people also have banners which are not flags. This one was carried before 1918 by American women who wanted the right to vote.

NEW FLAGS OF THE WORLD

On the following pages are stories of the flags of the countries that have declared their independence since the beginning of World War II. There are no flags here for countries that have had revolutions since 1939, if those countries were already independent at that time. Nor does the list include flags for Germany and China. Both of them were independent in 1939, but each now has two different governments ruling two different parts of the country.

ALGERIA (al-JEER-ee-uh): Ten million people, most of them Moslems, live in this country, which is three times the size of Texas. Algeria became an independent republic July 3, 1962. Before that time it had various rulers. Arabs conquered it in the seventh century. Then, beginning in 1518, it was ruled by Turks, and, beginning in 1830, by France. The French language is still permitted, but Arabic is the official language, replacing French in the schools. After independence was achieved, the National Assembly chose a flag that had first been used by revolutionaries in 1925. Notice that its crescent differs from crescents on the flags of Tunisia, Libya, Malaysia, Mauritania and some other Moslem countries. The longer horns of the crescent are supposed to bring better luck than shorter ones.

BOTSWANA (bah-TSWAH-nuh): In February, 1966, a group of people from Bechuanaland in southern Africa came to London. Together with representatives of the British government, they worked out plans for their country which was to become a republic under the name Botswana. September 30, 1966 was the date for independence. The original inhabitants of Botswana were Bushmen. About 24,000 of them still live there in the Kalahari Desert in very much the same way all human beings lived in the Old Stone Age. About 3,000 Europeans make their home in Botswana. The rest of the 550,000 people are Africans who belong to eight main tribes and who have their own religions. One out of seven is a Christian. The language called Tswana is widely spoken, but English is the official one.

When Botswana's Legislative Assembly chose its flag, it selected a colour combination not used by any of the tribes in the country. Blue represents the sky and the hope for water. Black stands for the majority of the people; white for the minority. The flag as a whole stands for tribal and racial equality and national unity.

BURMA (BURR-muh): In the eleventh century, Buddhist kings ruled this country in southeast Asia. Today, Buddhism is still the official religion. The Union of Burma is now a republic with certain socialist features. (Important industries, for example, are owned by the government.) Three-fourths of the 25,000,000 inhabitants speak some dialect of Burmese, the official language. English is also widely used by the government. One-fourth of the people belong to many different groups speaking many languages.

Beginning in 1612, the British took an interest in Burma. By 1886 they ruled the whole country, as well as neighbouring India. In 1937 they started work on a road which was to cross the mountains into China. These mountains are so steep that the road had to wind for 717 miles in order to go 204 miles as the crow flies. Later, supplies were sent over the Burma Road to help Chinese armies fight against invading Japanese armies. In 1942, Japan conquered Burma and the road was closed.

During World War II many Burmese fought against the Japanese, and these guerillas developed a flag with a big white star. In 1947, Burma became fully independent. On January 4, 1948, the big white star was put into the country's flag. The white stands for purity, truth and steadfastness. The smaller stars around the big one represent various minority groups. Blue is for the sky at night. Red is for courage, determination and unity.

In 1961 a Burmese Buddhist named U Thant became Acting Secretary-General of the United Nations. Later he became Secretary-General.

BURUNDI (boor-UN-dee): The kingdom of Burundi gained its independence from Belgium in 1962 and in that same year adopted a flag. The red in it stands for the sacrifices of those who fought for freedom. The green is for progress and prosperity, and the white stands for peace for all mankind. In the centre of the flag is a stalk of sorghum, an important crop in Burundi and a symbol of prosperity. Above the sorghum is a drum. Most of the 2,600,000 Burundians come from one of three tribes—the very tall Batusi (or Tutsi or Watusi), the very short Batwa (or Twa), and the medium-sized Bahutu (or Hutu). Each of these tribes has its own language.

CAMBODIA (KHMER REPUBLIC): In the year A.D. 80, the king of Cambodia chose a flag which was to be used with little change for almost 1900 years. However, when the king was deposed and Cambodia declared as the Khmer Republic in 1970, the flag was changed. It now features the twelfth century Buddhist temple, Angkor Wat, set in a red rectangle at the top left. Three white stars stand out against the blue of the rest of the flag to symbolise the Republic, Religion and the Principles of the Buddhism Philosophy.

The French seized Cambodia as a colony in 1863, but allowed the king to keep his throne. In 1947 he ceased to be an absolute monarch and began to rule under a constitution. In 1953 the country declared its independence from France. The 5,700,000 Cambodians speak Cambodian, also called Khmer, but many of the people also speak French, and some speak English. Buddhism is the official religion.

CAMEROON (kam-err-OON): This part of the western coast of Africa was the home of 200 independent tribes until Germany began to rule the

country in 1884. During World War I, in 1916, France took the eastern part of this colony from Germany and Britain took the western part. French Cameroon became independent on January 1, 1960. British Cameroon got its independence on October 1, 1961. The two parts of the country then united to form the Federal Republic of Cameroon and adopted their present flag. To the people of Cameroon, the green in the flag stands for hope and the tropical plants that grow in the southern part of the country. Red is the colour of authority and stands for the unity and independence of the two parts of the country. Yellow is for the soil of the North. It is also for wealth and for the sun, which Cameroonians say is the "source of the people's glory." Many African languages are spoken by the 6,000,000 people of the country. In East Cameroon, French is the official language for schools and the government; in the West, the official language is English.

CENTRAL AFRICAN REPUBLIC: About 1,400,000 people live just north of the Equator on the high-plateau land of this country. The area gained its independence from France on August 13, 1960. French remains the official language, but each of the four tribal groups of the country has its own tongue, and when people from two different tribes want to talk, they use a special language called Sangho. In 1958, as the country was preparing for independence, lawmakers approved a flag design unlike any other in existence: a vertical stripe running through four horizontal stripes.

CEYLON (SRI LANKA): In prehistoric times a group of Stone Age people moved onto this large island off the coast of India, and a few of their descendants still live there. Many other immigrants have arrived since then. The largest group, the Sinhalese, are believed to have come from northern India in the sixth century B.C. They kept their own language, and for a long time they had kings who flew a red flag with a yellow lion on it. Tamil people came from India with a different language, possibly in the fourteenth century. Moors, Malays, Portuguese and Dutch also invaded Ceylon. In 1796 the British overthrew the Dutch and ruled until 1948, when Ceylon became independent. About 6,000,000 people are Sinhalese who belong to the

Buddhist religion. About 1,000,000 Tamils are Hindus. There are also about 600,000 Christians and 400,000 Moslems. The flag of Ceylon, adopted in 1950, is the old flag of the Sinhalese kings. To it has been added a saffron stripe representing the Tamil-speaking group and a green stripe for the Moslems. Sinhalese is the official language, despite strong Tamil objections. Education from kindergarten through university is free. From 1960 to 1965, Mrs. Sirimavo Bandaranaike was prime minister, the first woman to hold this title.

CHAD: In 1959, Chad adopted a flag in which blue stands for the sky and for hope. Yellow is the colour of the sun which lights the land. Red is the colour of fire and symbolizes unity. In 1960, this country of 3,000,000 people ceased to be a colony of France and became independent. French is widely spoken and so are several tribal languages. People in the desert-like northern part of Chad are Moslems. In the wooded southern part, people follow several older African religions.

CONGO, THE REPUBLIC OF: This former French colony, with its capital at Brazzaville, gained independence on August 15, 1960, and became the Republic of Congo. It lies across the Congo River from the former Belgian colony now called the Democratic Republic of Congo. In 1965, it began to call itself a socialist country, and it adopted a one-party system of government. In 1959, as the country prepared for independence, its leaders adopted a flag which came into use a year later. The people—nearly 1,000,000—belong to several different tribes, including a small number of Pygmies. Each tribe has its own language. French is the official language of the government.

CONGO, THE DEMOCRATIC REPUBLIC OF (ZAIRE): In 1876, Leopold II, King of Belgium, started a company to carry on trading in a part of Africa through which the Congo River flows. For many years the king, acting as a private businessman, claimed ownership of this territory, an area much larger than the state of Texas. Then, in 1908, the Congo lands became a colony claimed by the Belgian government. In 1960, the 15,000,000 Congolese people won independence from Belgium and established a government they called the Democratic Republic of the Congo. Léopoldville became the country's capital. The constitution of the new government described what the country's flag should

be. The blue in it is for hope. Yellow is for prosperity. The star stands for the goal of the 200 tribes, which is unity, and the red stripe stands for the blood shed by Congolese as they sought that goal. About one-third of the Congolese are Roman Catholic; the rest follow African religions. The principal languages are Swahili and Lingala.

Leopoldville has now been re-named Kinshasa.

CYPRUS (SIGH-prus): Few countries on earth have had more foreign rulers than Cyprus. Powerful nations have wanted this island because ships from its ports could easily attack any other ships in the eastern part of the Mediterranean Sea. Whoever controlled Cyprus also controlled trade in that part of the world.

People also wanted Cyprus because of its copper mines. In fact, the word *copper* comes from the name *Cyprus*. Ancient Greeks may have been the first outsiders to conquer the island. Then came Phoenicians, Assyrians, Egyptians, Persians, Greeks again, Romans, Moslems, Crusaders, Venetians, Turks, and in 1878, the British. On August 16, 1960, after a fierce war, Cyprus won its independence from Britain and established a republic, with Archbishop Makarios of the Greek Orthodox Church as President. A Turk was named Vice-President. Four-fifths of the population are Greek-speaking Christians. One-fifth are Turkish-speaking Moslems. Most Cypriots, as both Greeks and Turks are called, also speak English. The flag, adopted in 1960, shows a map of Cyprus, under which are two olive branches symbolizing peace.

DAHOMEY (dah-HO-mee): This country had a long history as a kingdom with a large army. One feature of the army set it apart from all others: most of the soldiers were women, selected for their strength and great skill with weapons. After foreign traders reached Dahomey in the fifteenth century, the kings grew rich by selling slaves. During the nineteenth century, the French began to control Dahomey, and by 1895 the whole country was a French colony. It became an independent republic in 1960 and adopted its flag. Red is for the colour of the soil. Green is for the palm groves that abound in part of the land. Yellow is for the treeless plains, called savannas, in another part.

French is the official language of the government and schools, but the 2,105,000 Dahomeans are divided into a number of tribes, each of which has its own language.

GABON (gah-BAWN): This densely forested land on the west coast of Africa was the home of independent tribes until 1903, when France claimed it as a colony. The Gabon Republic was established in 1960 and adopted a flag. According to the government's figures, more than 80 per cent of the people can read and write French, the official language. Several different tribal languages are also spoken among the half-million Gabonese who include a small number of Pygmies. The famous advocate of peace, Dr. Albert Schweitzer, had a hospital here until his death in 1965.

GAMBIA (GAM-bee-uh): From the fifth to the eighth century, this country (always called *the* Gambia) was part of the great African empire of Ghana. Then it became part of Songhay, another African empire. In 1455, Portuguese ships looking for slaves explored the Gambia River, and Portuguese settlers began to live along its banks. These settlers intermarried with Gambians. Today, the only indications that Europeans once lived here are a few Portuguese names and customs. On Christmas Eve, for example, Christians and Moslems alike take part in a festival that began perhaps 500 years ago. Men dressed in fantastic naval uniforms parade in the streets, carrying ship models, some as long as twenty feet. These are really gigantic lanterns which have candles inside wooden frames covered with a lace-like paper cut out in elaborate designs. Cherry-coloured lanterns hang from the tops of the ships' masts. Paraders also carry models of houses, planes and automobiles as part of a celebration that lasts all night.

The British began to trade along the Gambia River in 1588 and the country became a British colony in 1821. On February 18, 1965, it became independent. The Gambia, smallest country in Africa, is shaped like a wrinkled stocking. It is surrounded by the former French colony of Senegal on three sides, and the Atlantic Ocean on the fourth. There are 324,000 Gambians who belong to several tribes, each of which keeps its own language. Five hundred Europeans also live here, and there is a colony of settlers from faraway Lebanon. The official language is English, which is used by the government and in many schools. The Moslems, who are numerous, have schools in which Arabic is taught. In the flag the red stripe at the top is for the sun. The blue is for the Gambia River. Green stands for agricultural resources, and the white stripes are for purity and peace.

GHANA (GAH-nuh): Between A.D. 800 and 1066 much of Europe was made up of tiny backward countries. At that same time, on the Niger River in Africa, there was a large, strong state called Ghana. This period in Africa's past was recalled on March 6, 1957. On that day, some distance away from the Niger River, people in Britain's Gold Coast Colony became independent, and they called their country Ghana. They liked the name, although the new republic of Ghana did not occupy any of the same territory as the old kingdom.

The red in the Ghanaian flag stands for those who worked for independence. The white is for victory in the struggle. Dark green represents the forests and farms of Ghana, and the black star is the guiding star of African freedom. The head of the government until 1966 was Kwame Nkrumah, who had been the leader in the fight for independence. The 17,500,000 Ghanaians belong to 87 different tribes, each with its own tongue. Seven of these are widely spoken, but the official language of the government and of most schools is English.

GUINEA (GHIN-ee): From the sixteenth to the nineteenth centuries European traders captured large numbers of Guineans for sale as slaves. In the nineteenth century, France gradually took control of the country, which had remained independent until then. Guinea regained its independence on October 7, 1958. A month later it adopted a flag. Red in the flag stands for blood shed in the struggle for freedom. Yellow stands for sunshine and for gold. Green represents the forests and vegetation of the country. About 3,500,000 people from a number of different tribes live in Guinea. Each tribe has its own language, but French is used in government business.

GUYANA (guy-ANN-uh): In 1581 the Dutch established the first European settlement in the country on the north coast of South America that is now called Guyana. In the next two centuries, the French, Portuguese and British all attempted to take the territory away from the Dutch, and in 1803 the British succeeded. For more than 150 years after that, it was called British Guiana (spelled with *i,* not a *y*). *Guiana* comes from an American Indian language. It means *land of waters*.

The original inhabitants were all American Indians. Today, their 30,000 descendants are called Amerindians, to distinguish them from 320,000 East Indians who live in Guyana and whose ancestors came from India. There are also 200,000 Guyanans who are descended from Africans, and many others whose ancestors were Chinese or Portuguese. English is the language of Guyana's government, its schools and of most of its people.

In preparation for independence, which came May 26, 1966, Guyana's House of Assembly chose a flag in which the green stands for the agriculture and forests of the country, the golden arrow represents mineral wealth, and a red triangle stands for the nation-building that lies ahead. A border of white stands for water resources and a black border for endurance that will be needed in the future.

Most Guyanans are Hindus, Moslems or Christians. Some of the Amerindians still follow their own religions.

ICELAND (ICE-land):

About 1,100 years ago, Norsemen from Norway moved into Iceland, an uninhabited volcanic island that they had found in the North Atlantic Ocean. In A.D. 930, settlers established a parliament called the *Althing,* which has been in existence ever since. This makes it the oldest parliament in the world. In 1262, Iceland joined Norway. Then, in 1380, both Norway and Iceland united with Denmark. Norway separated from Denmark in 1814, but Iceland did not. In 1918, Iceland became an independent country, except that she and Denmark shared the same king. Finally, in 1944, Iceland ended the monarchy and became a separate independent republic.

No country in the world has a higher percentage of people who can read and write, and probably no people in the world have more book stores. There is one for every thousand inhabitants. Children can and do read wonderful Icelandic stories exactly as they were written in the Middle Ages. This is possible because the Icelandic language has changed very little since then.

During the Middle Ages, when the many countries of Europe were fighting exhausting wars, Iceland was at peace. The country still has no army or navy. In the year 1000, the year in which the *Althing* adopted Christianity, an Icelandic explorer named Leif Erikson sailed to Vinland, on the coast of North America.

The Icelandic flag was adopted in 1916. It has the same design as the flag of Norway, but where the Norwegian flag is red, the Icelandic is blue, and vice versa. This in itself says clearly that Iceland is related to Norway, but also independent. The 187,000 Icelanders are Evangelical Lutherans.

INDIA (IN-dee-ah):

Nearly 500 million people live in this country which is so large that it is almost a continent by itself. Civilization in India goes back a long time. Five thousand years ago, people in the Indus Valley were building cities and using wheeled carts. They also had a form of writing, but nobody has discovered how to read it, so we don't know what language was spoken then. About half of the inhabitants of India today speak Hindi, the official language. English, as well as Hindi, is much used by the government. About a third of the people speak one of eleven other languages. The remainder belong to small groups that speak many languages. Most Indians follow the Hindu religion, but about 50,000,000 are Moslems, 10,000,000 are Christians and 8,000,000 are Sikhs.

The flag, which was adopted in 1947, when India won its independence from Britain, tells something of the country's history. In the centre is a wheel that has 24 spokes. This was an emblem used by a Buddhist king about 300 B.C. It is also a symbol for peaceful change. The white in the flag stands for simplicity and peace. The deep saffron means honesty and purity, and green stands for courage. The idea of peaceful change was taught by Mahatma Gandhi, who led India to freedom. He persuaded people that they should disobey Britain's laws — but without violence. These disobedience campaigns were very effective. After World War II, India gained independence. Gandhi's beliefs did not save him from violence. He was killed by an assassin a few months after India had won its freedom.

INDONESIA (in-doe-NEE-zhya):

According to tradition, a simple flag of red and white was used in the past in various parts of this country which consists of 3,000 islands. In the seventeenth century the Dutch made many of these islands into a colony. By 1927 Indonesians began to demand independence, and in 1929 the Indonesian National Movement adopted the traditional red and white flag as its own. During World War II the Japanese took Indonesia away from the Dutch. Then, in 1945, two days after the surrender of the Japanese, Indonesia declared its independence. In the same year it adopted the red and white flag that had been used by the National Movement — even

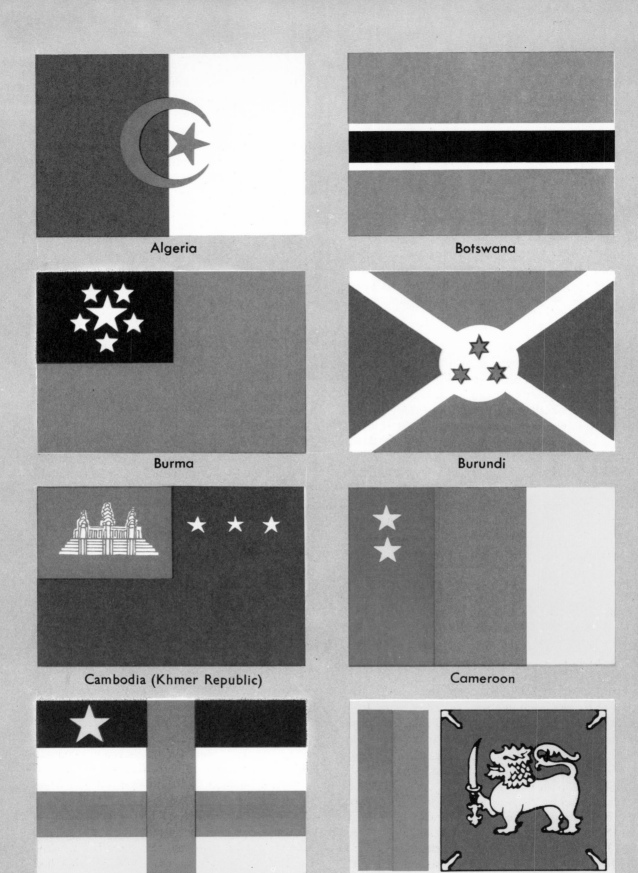

Algeria

Botswana

Burma

Burundi

Cambodia (Khmer Republic)

Cameroon

Central African Republic

Ceylon (Sri Lanka)

(In order to provide a uniform display, some of these
flags may vary slightly from their true proportions.)

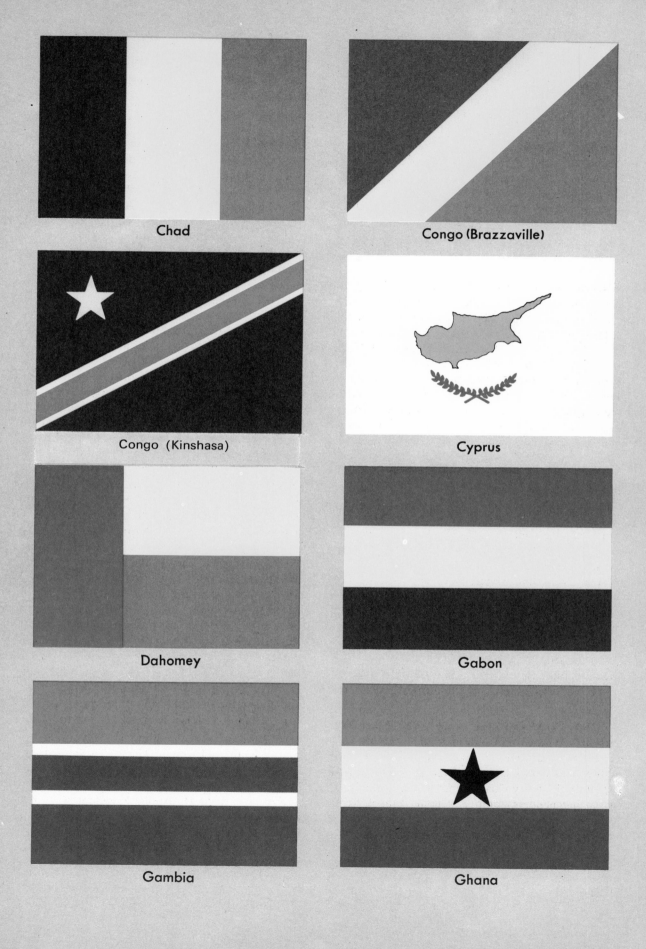

Chad

Congo (Brazzaville)

Congo (Kinshasa)

Cyprus

Dahomey

Gabon

Gambia

Ghana

though it happens to be the same as the one used by Monaco.

A great many different kinds of people make up the Indonesian population. They speak more than thirty different languages, and many of these languages have several dialects. But people from most of the islands can talk to each other in official Indonesian. This language developed out of Malay, the tongue used by traders who went from island to island. About 90,000,000 Indonesians are Moslems. Hindus, Buddhists and Christians total about 10,000,000, and there are some people who follow traditional religions of the islands.

ISRAEL (IS-rah-el): In A.D. 70, Romans destroyed the great temple of the Jews in Jerusalem and many of the people fled from their homeland. After that, they were often persecuted in the many countries of the world where they settled. During World War II the Nazis set out to kill every Jew in Germany and in the lands they conquered. Many Jews who survived wanted a homeland, and after the war the United Nations called for the formation of a Jewish state in the same area from which their ancestors had originally come. On May 15, 1948 (in the year 5708, according to the Jewish calendar), the state of Israel was established in what had formerly been called Palestine. Many Arabs already lived there, and Arabic is still taught in schools for Arabs. Hebrew is the language of most of the schools. Hundreds of thousands of Jews moved to Israel from Europe, America, Africa and Asia, but by 1965 about 40 per cent of the 2,400,000 Israelis were native-born. The six-pointed star in the Israeli flag is known as the Star (or shield) of David. Nobody is sure what meaning, if any, it originally had. Certainly it has been an important symbol in recent times, and from the ruins of the ancient city of Sidon, which was inhabited in the sixth century B.C., archaeologists excavated a design in the form of such a star.

IVORY COAST: So far as we know, Europeans first visited the Ivory Coast in West Africa in 1365. These explorers came from France — and France subsequently took control of the area. On August 7, 1960, the Ivory Coast Republic was established as an independent country, keeping French as its official language. Each of the five main tribal groups in the country has its own language and each of these in turn has several dialects. Nearly two-thirds of the 3,500,000 inhabitants follow the religions of their own tribal groups. About 14 per cent are Christians and 23 per cent are Moslems. The Ivory Coast has perhaps the highest birth and death rates in the world.

JAMAICA (juh-MAY-kuh): This island was discovered by Christopher Columbus in 1494 when it was inhabited by Arawak Indians. The last of these Indians died or were killed while Jamaica was a Spanish colony. The British captured the island in 1655, and for many years it was a headquarters for pirates. British rule lasted until 1962. Then the island became independent with a parliamentary form of government. The black in its flag stands for hardships, partly overcome but partly still to be faced. Gold is for natural wealth and the beauty of sunlight. Green is for hope and agricultural resources. Taken all together, the flag means this: "Hardships there are, but the land is green and the sun shines." Many of the 1,700,000 Jamaicans are descended from African slaves. Settlers have also come from Europe, India and China, and much intermarriage has taken place between Jamaicans of different origins. Many of the people speak a dialect of English, and English is the language of the government and the schools.

JORDAN (JOR-dan): Jericho, the oldest town in the world, is in this very old country. So are many places important in the history of Jewish, Christian and Islamic religions. Before World War I, the area was part of the Ottoman (Turkish) Empire. When the Turks, allies of the Germans, were defeated, Britain was given supervision of Jordan. The country became independent in 1946. It adopted, later with a change, a flag that had once been used by Hejaz, a former desert kingdom. Hejaz had become a part of Saudi Arabia and no longer flew a flag of its own. The colours in the flag have great meaning for Moslems who are the majority of the 1,700,000 Jordanians. Black, white and green each stands for a family important in early Islamic history. Red stands for the Great Arab Revolution — the effort of all Arabs to cooperate with each other. The seven-pointed star represents seven verses of the Koran, the holy book of the Moslems. The official name of this new country is the Hashemite Kingdom of Jordan. Hashem is the name of a prominent Moslem family. Hussein I, who became king in 1952, is a member of the family, and traces his ancestry to Mohammed. Arabic is the official language.

KENYA (KENN-ya): By the eighth century Arab traders had visited the part of East Africa that is now called Kenya. In the fifteenth century, Vasco da Gama, the Portuguese explorer, reached the country. For a long time after that, Arabs and Portuguese fought against each other and against the Kenyans, many of whom they seized and sold as slaves. In the nineteenth century, Britain gained control of the area. In 1953, a Kenyan organization known as the Mau Mau began a ferocious struggle against the British, who replied by jailing 60,000 Kenyans including Jomo Kenyatta, leader of the revolution. When Kenya won independence in 1963, Kenyatta became Prime Minister.

The 9,100,000 Kenyans come from about fifty tribes, of which the largest is the Kikuyu. When members of two different tribes want to talk to each other, they speak Swahili, which is an international tongue in much of Africa. English is the official language of the government. Both English and Swahili are taught in schools.

Among the non-Africans in Kenya are about 150,000 Asians, partly Moslem, partly Hindu; about 50,000 Europeans, mostly British Christians; and about 30,000 Arab Moslems. In the north there are Somalis who want to secede and join Somalia.

In 1963, Kenya adopted a flag that has a big African shield in its centre. Behind it are crossed spears called *assegais*.

KOREA (SOUTH and NORTH): For many centuries the emperors of Korea would not let foreigners enter the country, and Koreans could not travel abroad. Then, in 1872, Emperor Kojong decided to make a change. Korea stopped being the Hermit Kingdom and began to trade with other countries. For the first time it felt the need for a flag. Government officials collected designs from which the Emperor chose one that became official. The background was white, which stands for peace. (Koreans are so fond of white, they are often called *the white-clad people*.) The circle in the centre divided by an S-shaped line, represents many things. First of all, it symbolizes the idea that there are two sides to everything — good and evil, male and female, night and day, and so on. The red half

of the circle stands for the sun, the blue half for the moon. The designs made of black bars are called Divine Designs. They also are full of meaning. For example, long bars outside short bars mean that those who are stronger should protect those who are weaker. Short bars outside a long bar mean that the one who is most precious (the long bar) should be protected by those who are less important (the small bars). The meanings of this flag are practically endless, and Koreans say it is supposed to make people think about the meaning of the whole universe. The design itself was based on four principles of the Confucian religion.

The Kingdom of Korea flew this flag until the country was seized as a colony of Japan in 1910. During World War II, Britain, the United States, China and the Soviet Union agreed that Korea should be independent after the war. Then, by agreement among them, Soviet troops occupied the northern part of Korea and the United States troops occupied the southern part. In May, 1948, the Republic of Korea was formed in South Korea and adopted the flag almost exactly like the old one. In the same month the People's Democratic Republic of Korea was established in North Korea and adopted a separate flag. This included the five-pointed star that appears on flags of several countries governed by communists.

About 28,000,000 people live in South Korea. About 11,000,000 live in North Korea. Many are Confucians, Buddhists, Christians and believers in the Chondogyo religion. The language is Korean.

KUWAIT (koo-WITE): About 300 years ago, Arab tribes from central Arabia moved to the shore at the head of the Arabian gulf. There they became fishermen, shipbuilders and merchants. In 1889, Britain began to direct the foreign affairs of this little country. Then, in 1934, a great change took place in the life of the people, who are Moslems and ruled by a monarch called the Emir. A rich oil field was discovered, and immense wealth poured into Kuwait. The government says that its 400,000 citizens receive the highest incomes in the world. Medical care is free. So is education. By 1965, 60 percent of the people could read and write. When Kuwait became independent in 1961, the Emir decreed a new flag. The green in it stands for hope that agriculture may develop in this desert land (a real possibility, with irrigation). Kuwait has built a huge plant that is changing sea water

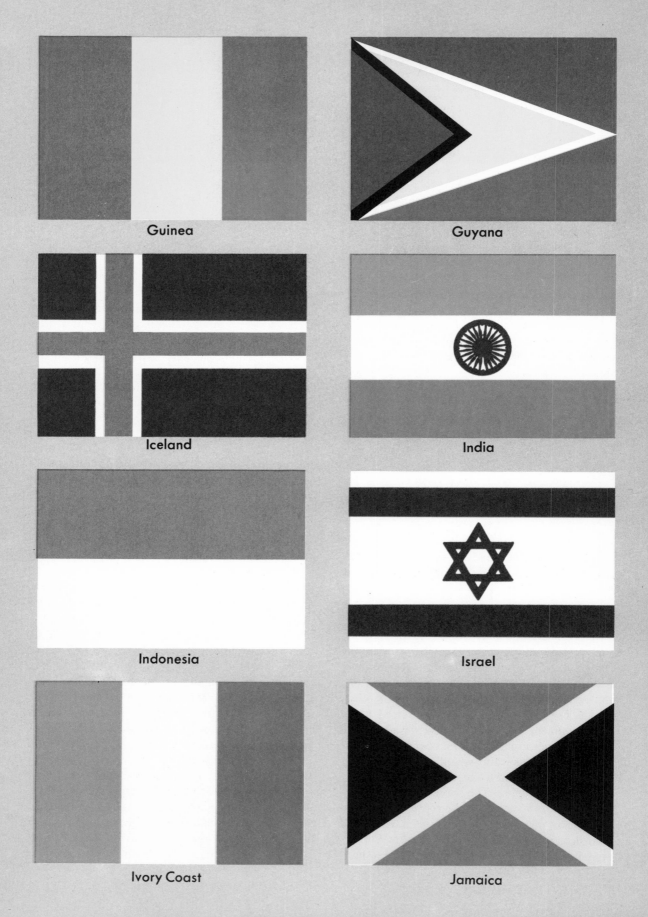

Guinea

Guyana

Iceland

India

Indonesia

Israel

Ivory Coast

Jamaica

(In order to provide a uniform display, some of these
flags may vary slightly from their true proportions.)

Jordan

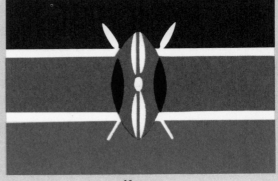

Kenya

Korea — North

Korea — South

Kuwait

Laos

Lebanon

Libya

into fresh water. White in the flag stands for the big achievements of this little country. Red stands for traditional horsemanship and swordsmanship, and black is for bravery in war.

LAOS (LOUZ): The Kingdom of Laos was founded in the thirteenth century and was once called Lanxang, which means *Land of a Million Elephants*. In 1893, France made Laos into a part of the French empire. By 1954, the 3,000,000 Laotians had gained full independence as a constitutional monarchy. Many of the officials and city dwellers speak French, but the official language is Lao. The religion of the country is Buddhism. The three-headed elephant on the flag stands for three parts of the ancient kingdom united into one. The white parasol is the symbol of monarchy. The stairway stands for the first five commandments of Buddhism: Do not kill; do not steal; do not lie; do not covet thy neighbour's wife; do not abuse the use of liquor.

LEBANON (LEB-uh-nun): For a long time before the end of World War I, this country was ruled by Turkey. Then France supervised the government of Lebanon for a number of years. In 1943, Lebanese patriots designed a flag that their country could use as soon as it was free. Independence came in 1944. The red in the flag stands for sacrifice. The white stands for peace. The tree in the center symbolizes strength, holiness and eternity. It is the cedar of Lebanon, which has been famous around the Mediterranean Sea for nearly 5,000 years. The pharaohs of Egypt sent ships for the huge cedar logs to make beams in their buildings. King Solomon, according to the Bible, had "fourscore thousand hewers in the mountains," cutting the cedars for his temple in Jerusalem. So many of the trees were chopped down that the great forests of Lebanon were destroyed and its hills left bare. Only a few of the cedars have survived, but they are now protected by the Lebanese government. No one may cut them without permission.

In this land of about 2,000,000 people, the language is Arabic. The president must be a Christian and the prime minister a Moslem. This reflects the division of the population, half-and-half between the two religions.

LIBYA (LIB-ya): This North African land, where 1,270,000 Arab Moslems live, was the first country to receive its full independence under plans made by the United Nations. Before independence, Libya had been ruled by Benito Mussolini as part of his Italian empire. In 1951, Libya became a constitutional monarchy and adopted a flag. The red is for the blood shed in battles that are past. Green represents the farms. The crescent moon reminds Libyans that they are Moslems. The five-pointed star stands for hope, belief in God and love of country. Black is for an important Moslem family.

MALAGASY REPUBLIC (mal-uh-GAHS-ee ree-PUB-lick): About 1810, the French and British began to compete with each other for the control of Madagascar, a large island off the east coast of Africa. By 1885 the French had won out. They ruled the island until 1960, when it became the Malagasy Republic. At that time there was a contest for a design for a national flag. In the winning design white stands for purity, red for independence and green for hope. The 6,300,000 Malagasy are a mixture of Polynesians, Africans and Arabs. Their language is related to the languages of Malaysia and Polynesia, but French is taught in the schools. About 1,000,000 Malagasy are Catholics; the same number are Protestants. The rest follow the ancient religions of the people.

MALAWI (mah-LAH-wee): About 3,800,000 Africans, 8,000 Europeans and 12,000 people from India live in this republic. One border is on the shore of Lake Nyasa, where high forested mountains rise steeply. Elsewhere there are level plains. Europeans first saw this land of great contrasts in 1859. Later, it became a British colony called Nyasaland. In July, 1964, it achieved independence, adopted the name Malawi, and chose a flag. The black in the flag stands for all Africans. The rising sun represents the dawn of hope and freedom in Africa. Red is for the blood of Africans who have given their lives for freedom. Green is for the vegetation of Malawi, which stays green the year round.

MALAYSIA (mah-LAY-zhya): From early in the nineteenth century, Britain ruled the Malay Peninsula in Southeast Asia. Eleven separate colonies made up the Federation of Malay States, and in most of the states hereditary sultans governed with the approval of the British. These colonies joined with three others in September, 1963, formed a new country and elected a king. The flag of this new country was based on the one used by Malaya, the largest of the states. In the new flag were fourteen stripes, one for each of the former colonies. The star had fourteen points. It was yellow, a symbol of royalty. The crescent stood for the religion of the Moslems.

Although several languages are spoken in Malaysia, most people can talk to each other in Malay. English is a required subject in the schools. At the time of independence, 42 per cent of the 9,000,000 Malaysians were Chinese; 40 per cent were Malays and related peoples; the rest came from India, Pakistan and other countries. In 1965, Singapore, one of the fourteen states of Malaysia, seceded and became a separate country.

MALDIVE ISLANDS (MAL-dive EYE-lands): Long ago, people from the island of Ceylon began to live on some of the 200 tiny coral Maldive Islands more than 400 miles away. The Maldivians were Buddhists until 1153, when they were persuaded to become Moslems. Portuguese captured the islands in the sixteenth century, but were finally driven out. The islands remained independent until 1887. Then they became part of the British colonial system. In 1965, they regained their independence under the rule of a sultan.

The language of the 95,000 Maldivians is related to Sinhalese, which is spoken by part of the people of Ceylon. English is also much used and studied in schools, including schools for girls which were recently started.

Through most of the 800 years since Maldivians were converted to the Islamic faith, their flag was pure red with no design on it. Then a prime minister, who has been called the Mussolini of the Maldives, changed the flag to its present form. He did this, it is said, because he thought red had become associated with communism. The red in the new flag stands for the blood the Maldivians shed to get their national freedom. Green is for peace and prosperity, and the crescent is a Moslem emblem.

MALI (MOLL-ee): The Republic of Mali is a large plain in West Africa. Its 4,500,000 people come from many different tribes and speak many different languages. One important language, Bambara, now has an alphabet and can be written, as can several others. The official language for the whole country is French, which is also used in schools.

A vigorous empire called Mali developed in West Africa in the thirteenth century and lasted till late in the fifteenth century. Then another empire called Songhay replaced it, lasting until Moslem armies from the north destroyed it in the sixteenth century. In the nineteenth century the French invaded the country and turned it into a colony. On September 22, 1960, Mali became an independent socialist republic. The next year it adopted a flag. Yellow in the flag stands for purity and the country's natural resources. Red is for courage and the blood shed in the fight for independence. Green is for the vegetation in this agricultural country. Most of the people are Moslems.

MALTA (MAWL-tuh): This island in the Mediterranean Sea has been ruled by Phoenicians, Greeks, Romans, Carthaginians, Arabs, Sicilians, French and English. According to tradition, Count Roger, a Crusader from Normandy, landed on Malta in 1094 to drive out the Arabs. The Maltese welcomed Roger, and he rewarded them by giving them part of his coat of arms to use in their flag. This part consisted of the colors white and red.

From 1530 to 1798 Malta was independent and was ruled by a Christian military organization sometimes called the Knights of Malta. The French general Napoleon took the island away from the Knights. The British then took it away from Napoleon in 1802. During World War II Malta held out against strong German bombing, and in 1942 King George VI awarded the Cross of St. George to the island for the heroism of its people. When Malta attained independence in 1964, this cross was placed on the flag, which also had the red and white colours supposedly going back to the year 1094.

The Maltese have their own language, based on the Semitic languages of the Arabs and the ancient Carthaginians, with many Italian words added. Children in the elementary grades learn in Maltese. In the last years of high school they study English, and then use English in the university. The government conducts its business in both Maltese and English, but Maltese is the official language. Most Maltese are Roman Catholics.

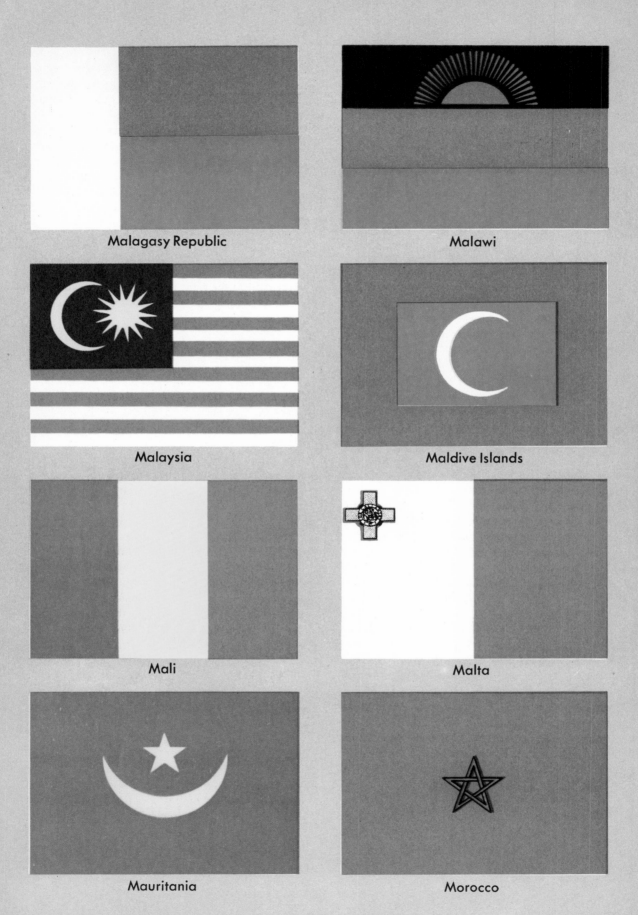

Malagasy Republic

Malawi

Malaysia

Maldive Islands

Mali

Malta

Mauritania

Morocco

(In order to provide a uniform display, some of these flags may vary slightly from their true proportions.)

Niger

Nigeria

Pakistan

Philippines

Rhodesia

Rwanda

Senegal

Sierra Leone

MAURITANIA (mor-uh-TAIN-ya): In 1960, a French colony in West Africa won independence and took the name Islamic Republic of Mauritania. Its flag is made up of symbols often associated with Islam, the religion of Moslems. One of these is the color green, which also stands for prosperity and hope. Other symbols are the star and crescent.

Mauritanians who have Negro ancestors live peacefully with Moors whose ancestors were Arabs and Berbers. There are about 1,000,000 Mauritanians altogether, and most of them make their living as farmers or fishermen. The government believes that many people will become industrial workers when their country begins to use its iron ore deposits, which are among the largest in the world. Three-fourths of the people can read and write, according to government figures. Arabic is the language of the people, but French is used by the government.

MOROCCO (moh-ROCK-oh): This country, which became independent in 1956, is a relic of the Arab empire that covered northwest Africa and most of Spain and Portugal in the eighth century. At that time Islam, the religion of Mohammed, was brought to Morocco, and most of the 15,000,000 Moroccans today are Moslems. There are also Catholics. Some of them live in the part of Morocco that once belonged to the French empire, others in an area once controlled by Spain. Most Moroccans are descended from Arabs, but about 2,000,000 are Berbers whose ancestors were living in the country when the Arabs arrived. In the cities and towns near the coast there are a good many Jews. Some of their ancestors settled there more than 2,000 years ago. Others arrived in the fifteenth century, when all Jews who would not join the Catholic Church were forced to leave Spain.

Spanish and French are taught in private schools. The Berbers speak a language of their own which has several dialects. The official language is Arabic, taught in a few religious schools. There is no compulsory education. Most Moroccans can neither read nor write.

The ancestors of the present king adopted an all-red flag in the seventeenth century. Then, in 1912, when France took control of the country, a five-pointed star was added to distinguish the Moroccan flag from others that were plain red. The same flag is still used today.

NIGER (NYE-juhr): France once ruled the 3,200,-000 people of this West African country, which became an independent republic August 3, 1960. About 95 per cent of the people are Moslems. They come from many tribes and speak many languages, only one of which has been written. French is the official language of the government. Three-fourths of the people are farmers in the southern part of the country. The other fourth are nomads who wander over the Sahara Desert in the north. Many of the nomads are Tuaregs who in former times were warriors. Now they are busy organizing caravans or raising livestock. The flag was adopted in 1959, before independence. Its orange disc stands for the sun. The green stripe represents the fertile southern part of the country. The orange stripe is for the desert, and the white stands for purity.

NIGERIA (nye-JEER-ee-uh): One-fifth of all the people of Africa — 55,000,000 — live in the Federal Republic of Nigeria, which won its independence on October 1, 1960. Before that, this land was ruled by Britain. English is the official language, but there are nearly 250 tribes in the country, and each one has its own language and religious traditions. The most widespread religion is Islam. In 1959, as independence drew near, there was a national contest for a flag design. The winner, among 2,870 Nigerians who submitted designs, was a young engineer, Tadwo Ahinkunni. The green in the flag stands for fertile agricultural land, the white for peace and purity.

PAKISTAN AND BANGLADESH: The state of Pakistan came into existence as a dominion within the Commonwealth in August 1947, under the leadership of Mohammed Ali Jinnah, with Liaquat Ali Khan as its first prime minister. In 1964 Pakistan gave a new symbolic meaning to the flag. The white represents peace. Green is for prosperity. The crescent stands for progress, and the star represents light and knowledge. Pakistan was divided into a Western and an Eastern section, the two separated by over 1,000 miles of Indian territory.

In December 1971 India's victory over Pakistan resulted in East Pakistan, or Bangladesh, being established as an independent country. Sheikh

Mujibur Rahman became the first prime minister. The flag of Bangladesh shows a rising sun on a dark green background.

People in Bangladesh speak Bengali, and those in Pakistan speak Urdu, a language brought to the area by the Hindu servants of Mongol conquerors in the twelfth and thirteenth centuries. The majority of Pakistanis are Muslim, while the people of Bangladesh are predominantly Hindu. The latter, though smaller in area, is far more densely populated.

PHILIPPINES (FILL-uh-peens): The first European visit to the Philippine Islands was made in 1521 by the Portuguese explorer Ferdinand Magellan. Spanish explorers came later, and gradually the Philippines became a Spanish colony. In the 1890's, Filipinos organized a revolution against their Spanish rulers and adopted various flags, most of which had a triangle as a symbol. The leader of the revolution, General Emilio Aguinaldo, designed the one that was raised when the Philippines declared their independence from Spain in 1898. This flag did not fly long, because the United States invaded the Philippines, fought against the revolutionaries, and began to rule the country. During World War II the Japanese occupied the Philippines for three years. After the war, in 1946, the country became independent and again began to use the flag that Aguinaldo had designed nearly fifty years before. The old general was still living. The white triangle in the flag stands for the revolution of the 1890's. The eight rays of the sun stand for the first eight provinces that rebelled against Spain. Three stars represent the three main groups of the islands. Red stands for courage, blue for high political ideals, white for purity and peace. In time of peace, the blue stripe is flown at the top. In time of war, the red is on top.

The official language of the Philippine Republic is Tagalog, one of 84 used by the country's 30,-000,000 people. Only 45 per cent of all Filipinos speak it. English and Spanish are also official.

RHODESIA (ro-DEE-zhya): In 1965, 217,000 Europeans in this African country declared their independence from Britain. They did this to avoid giving equal rights to the 4,000,000 African Rhodesians. Later, in 1968, Rhodesia adopted a new flag, vertically striped, green, white, green. In the centre of the flag, appear the national arms: a pair of sable antelopes supporting a shield in which a pick, representing the mining industry, is shown. The crest, of gold, is one of the soapstone figurines of a bird discovered in the ruined city of Zimbabwe. Below the bird and enclosed in the shield is a lion with a thistle on each side. These came from the coat of arms of Cecil Rhodes, an Englishman from whom Rhodesia gets its name. Rhodes went to southern Africa in the 1800's and saw what enormous wealth in diamonds and gold could be mined in that part of the world. He and many other powerful men believed that a strong country had a right to take over weaker ones if it could, so he helped his government annex southern Africa to the British empire.

RWANDA (ruh-WAHN-dah): For a long time, farmers who belonged to the Hutu tribe were the main inhabitants of this beautiful mountain country in Africa. Alongside the farmers lived a small group of hunters called Twa who are relatives of the Pygmies. Then three or four hundred years ago a tribe of very tall people called Tutsi (or Batusi or Watusi) invaded the country from the direction of Ethiopia. The Tutsi had herds of big-horned cattle and were fierce warriors. Although the Hutu outnumbered them ten to one, the Hutu and Twa were very soon ruled by the Tutsi. The Hutu had to take care of the conquerors' cattle. A man who owned many cattle had a great deal of influence, and cattle are still important. A Rwandian won't eat vegetables at the same meal at which he drinks milk. He believes that if he does he may bring harm to the cows that produce the milk.

In 1885, the big countries in Europe divided faraway Africa into colonies. Germany got Rwanda and held it until she was defeated in World War I. Then the victorious nations gave Rwanda to Belgium, which had the Tutsi rule the country for them. After World War II, the Hutu majority began to revolt against the Tutsi and the Belgians. At the end of this civil war, the Hutu won a nationwide election and, on July 1, 1962, declared the independence of Rwanda. The flag had already been adopted on January 28, 1961. The red in it stands for the bloodshed and suffering endured to achieve freedom. Yellow is for victory of the revolution. Green is for hope, and *R* is for Rwanda.

Ninety per cent of the people of Rwanda are

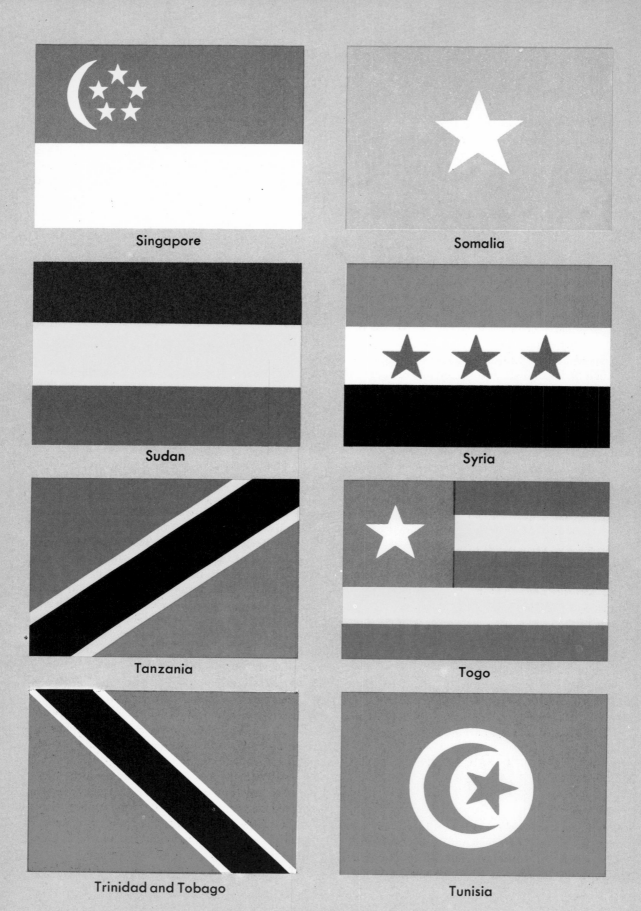

Singapore

Somalia

Sudan

Syria

Tanzania

Togo

Trinidad and Tobago

Tunisia

(In order to provide a uniform display, some of these flags may vary slightly from their true proportions.)

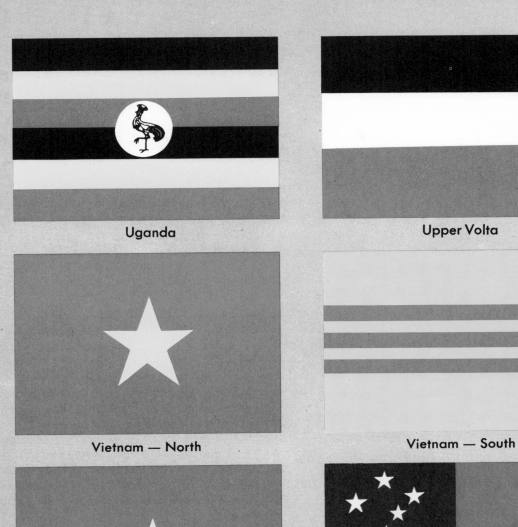

Uganda

Upper Volta

Vietnam — North

Vietnam — South

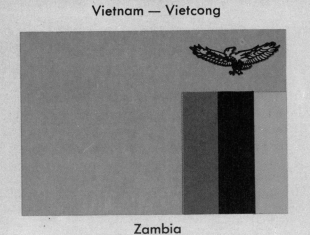

Vietnam — Vietcong

Western Samoa

Zambia

United Nations

Hutu, 9 per cent are Tutsi and less than 1 per cent are Twa. The national language is Kinyarwanda, but French is also official. More than half of the people practice the religions of their own tribes. About 37 per cent are Roman Catholics, and about 6 per cent are Protestants.

SENEGAL (sen-eh-GAHL): This republic with a population of 3,500,000 was ruled by the French from 1815 to 1958, when it became independent. The next year it joined in a federation with the country now called Mali. Then, in 1960, these two countries separated. The Senegalese speak several tribal languages, but French is official. When Senegal parted from Mali, it continued to use the colors of the flag of the federation, but added a five-pointed green star. The star stands for man. In 1966, a month-long World Festival of Negro Artists was held in Senegal. Negro poets, painters, musicians — artists of all kinds — came to the Festival from all over Africa and the Americas.

SIERRA LEONE (see-AIR-uh lee-OWN): About 2,200,000 people live in this former British colony on the west coast of Africa. English is the official language. Thirteen different tribal languages are spoken, and two of these are written. The name of the country, meaning *Mountain of the Lion,* was what Portuguese sailors called the mountain range along the coast which always seemed to be surrounded by fierce thunderstorms. Freetown, the capital city, was established in 1797 as a home for freed slaves. It now has a population of 50,000, a great many of whom are descendants of the original settlers.

On April 26, 1961, Sierra Leone became independent, and its flag, which had been selected in a competition, was raised for the first time. Green is for the vegetation of this agricultural country. White is for peace, and blue is for the nearby ocean. Many of the people in Sierra Leone practice the religions of their tribes. About one-third are Moslems. A slightly smaller number have been converted to Christianity.

SINGAPORE (SING-ah-pohr): On August 9, 1965, the island-city of Singapore withdrew from the new country of Malaysia, became an independent republic. Its state flag became the national flag. The red stripe stands for universal brotherhood and equality of man. The white means everlasting purity and virtue. The shape of the new moon on the flag suggests that Singapore is a new country, just beginning. The five stars stand for democracy, peace, progress, justice and equality. The original population of Singapore was Malay, and the Malay tongue remains the national language. However, two-thirds of the people are now Chinese, and Chinese is also an official language. The Tamil language, spoken by many Indians, is also official, and so is English, which is widely used in government work. All religions are permitted. The six largest are Islam, Christianity, Buddhism, Hinduism, Confucianism and Taoism.

SOMALIA (soh-MAHL-yah): Nearly 5,000,000 Somalis, many of whom are Moslems, live in an area of eastern Africa that is divided into five regions. The five-pointed star on the flag of the Somali Republic stands for these five regions. Two of them were formerly colonies held by Britain and Italy. They were supervised by the United Nations after World War II and achieved their independence in 1960. In 1954, when the Somalis were getting ready for independence, they chose their flag, using the white and blue of the United Nations flag. Three areas where Somalis live are still under foreign rule: French Somaliland, part of Ethiopia and a part of Kenya.

Almost everyone in Somalia speaks the Somali language, but it has not yet been written down. The official languages in which the government does business are English, Italian and Arabic. Arabic is the language of the schools. The constitution of the Somali Republic specifies that its president must be a Moslem.

SUDAN (soo-DAN): This country of 14,000,000 people lies south of Egypt along the Nile River and its tributaries. Arabs who are Moslems live in the northern part of Sudan. The official language of the country and its schools is Arabic, except for the university, where teaching is in English. A number of Negro tribes, each with its own religion and language, live in the southern part of the country. In 1820-22, the ruler of Egypt conquered the Sudan, and Egypt governed the area for nearly sixty years. Gordon who was given the task of withdrawing British garrisons, was killed at Khartoum in 1885 by the besieging forces of the Mahdi, who had destroyed General Hicks's army in 1883.

In 1896, British and Egyptian forces joined together to regain control of the Sudan, and by 1898 they had succeeded. From then until 1951, Egypt and Britain jointly ruled the country. The Egyptian and British flags flew side by side on all government buildings. The Sudan became independent on January 1, 1956. At that time the Republic of the Sudan adopted a flag that stood for the kind of country in which the Sudanese live. Blue is for the Nile River. Yellow is for the irrigated sands of the desert, and green is for the crops.

SYRIA (SEER-yuh): The ancient land of Syria was ruled by Turkey from 1516 until Turkey was defeated in World War I. France then took over control and ruled until January 1, 1944, when Syria became fully independent. Syria was part of the United Arab Republic from 1958 to 1961. Then it seceded and became the Syrian Arab Republic, adopting the present flag. The three stars in the flag stand for Arab revolutions. The green stripe represents the traditional colour of one group of Moslem leaders called the Orthodox Caliphs. White was the colour of another group, the Omayyad Caliphs. Black was the colour of the Abbasid Caliphs. The majority of the 5,500,000 Syrians are Moslems and the official language of the country is Arabic. There are also many Christians.

TANZANIA (tan-zan-EE-uh): The oldest fossil human bones ever found come from Tanganyika, which is part of Tanzania. This means that the human race may have begun there more than 2,000,000 years ago. If this is so, the very new country of Tanzania has a longer human story than any other country in the world.

Arabs began to settle in Tanganyika in the eighth century, but for more than a thousand years the country remained the home of independent tribes. Germany seized part of it in 1885, but lost it in World War I. The British ruled after that, until Tanganyika became independent in 1961.

Zanzibar, also part of Tanzania, is an island off the coast of Africa. The Portuguese ruled it from about 1500 to about 1700. Arabs from the Sultanate of Muscat then ruled until 1856, when Zanzibar became independent under the rule of a Sultan. In 1890, by agreement among the big European countries, Britain added Zanzibar to her colonial empire. The island again became an independent Sultanate in 1963, but a revolution overthrew the Sultan in 1964. The following year, Zanzibar and

Tanganyika united, forming Tanzania. In the flag they adopted, black stands for the people. Green is for the land. Yellow is for the country's wealth. Blue represents the sea. Ten million people live in Tanzania. They belong to about 125 tribes with almost as many languages and dialects. Swahili is their official language, and both Swahili and English are taught in the schools.

TOGO (TOE-go): When countries in Europe began to rule different parts of Africa, a long, narrow strip of land now called Togo in West Africa came under control of Germany. During World War I, Germany lost this territory, and after 1922 the French ruled it. Then, in 1960, Togo became an independent republic. In its flag, green stands for hope and for agriculture. (About 90 per cent of the Togolese are farmers.) Yellow stands for faith in the importance of their work. Red is the color of charity, faithfulness, love and sacrifice for humanity. White is the symbol of purity.

TRINIDAD and TOBAGO (TRIN-i-dad; toh-BAY-go): Columbus discovered Trinidad in 1498. This island, together with the nearby island of Tobago, was ruled by the British from 1802 until 1962, when independence came to the 1,000,000 English-speaking Trinidadeans. (That is what the inhabitants of both islands are called.) Calypso singing and band instruments made from empty oil drums may have begun in music-loving Trinidad. Its national flag, which came into use on the first day of independence, was selected by the cabinet and is unusually full of symbolic meanings. Black represents the devotion of Trinidadeans to national unity. White stands for the sea around the islands, for the purity of the people's hopes and for the equality of all men. Red is for the vitality of the people and of their land. It also stands for friendliness and for the warmth and energy of the sun.

About 440,000 of the people are Negro, 360,000 are East Indians and 170,000 are Lebanese or Syrian. There are about 700,000 Christians on the islands, both Roman Catholic and Protestant; 230,000 people follow the Hindu religion and 60,000 are Moslems.

TUNISIA (too-NEEZH-yuh): Nearly 3,000 years ago, merchants and mariners from Phoenicia on the eastern shore of the Mediterranean Sea built the city of Carthage on the north coast of Africa in what is now Tunisia. These Phoenicians brought with them two symbols that were popular in their country and in Greece: the star and the crescent. Much later, Moslem Arabs conquered Tunisia, and they, too, used these symbols. Still later, Turks conquered the country. They were Moslems and the crescent was important to them. The red flag of Turkey flew over Tunisia until 1881, when the country became part of the French empire. In 1956, Tunisia won independence and adopted a constitution similar in many ways to that of the United States. A flag with a star and crescent was chosen to remind Tunisians of their three-thousand-year history. Its red background comes from the long period when Tunisia was part of the Turkish empire.

Soon after Tunisia became a new, separate nation, each of its nearly 4,000,000 inhabitants received a family name. Until then, most Tunisians did not have names that identified them very clearly. A man might be called Mohammed ben Ahmed ben Mohammed, but this is only a given name meaning Mohammed, who is the son of Ahmed, who is the son of Mohammed. A law requiring every Tunisian to have a family name was made effective in 1959.

After independence, Arabic became the official language of the government and the schools. However, some French is still taught. Back in 1885, only 732 boys and six girls attended school in Tunisia, but after two years of independence, 230,-000 boys were in public schools, and 110,000 girls.

UGANDA (yoo-GAHN-da): This country borders on Lake Victoria, second largest lake in the world and source of the Nile River. Uganda lies across the Equator, but it has glaciers on its very high peaks which are called the Mountains of the Moon. The 7,000,000 Ugandans are themselves as full of variety as their country. Dozens of tribes live there, each with its own language and customs. Twelve of the languages have been written down, and there are daily radio programs in ten of them. Luganda is the most widely spoken. Swahili is also well-known.

Members of the different tribes seldom intermarry, and within the tribes are clans whose members almost never marry each other. Kings, whose powers are limited by a constitution, rule in different districts.

In the latter part of the nineteenth century, Britain took over control of Uganda. After that, Moslem, Protestant and Catholic missionaries all gained converts among Ugandans, and religious competition became keen. Fighting actually broke out between Catholics and Protestants, and in 1892 they had a serious battle. From time to time some of the tribes also have fought each other.

A crested crane was used as a symbol for Uganda when it was a British colony. This bird was put on the flag of Uganda when the country became independent.

UPPER VOLTA (UP-per VOHL-ta): About 800 years ago a warlike band of horsemen invaded the African land now known as Upper Volta and established themselves as masters over a large population of peaceful farmers. The rules that the conquerors made were very strict, and customs developed that made it easy for a few to rule over many.

In 1897, France took control of this area which gets its name from three main branches of the Volta River flowing through it. The flag reflects the importance of these rivers, too. Black is for the Black Volta; white is for the White Volta; and red is for the Red Volta. The flag was adopted in 1959, when the country was preparing for independence, which came in 1960. The 4,500,000 Upper Voltans belong to many tribes and speak many languages, but the official one is French. Half of all the people in this country are under twenty years of age.

VIETNAM (vee-EHT-nahm): More than 2,000 years ago, some people known as Viets were driven out of central China and settled in Southeast Asia, which China controlled during long periods afterward. Europeans arrived in the sixteenth century, and by 1884, France held all of the area now called Vietnam. The Japanese seized this country during World War II and set up a government headed by Emperor Bao Dai which, in 1945, chose the flag still used today by the Republic of Vietnam, whose headquarters are in Saigon. Also in 1945, the Democratic Republic of Vietnam declared its independence and established its capital in the city of Hanoi.

The French returned to Vietnam after Japan had been defeated, but the Vietnamese resisted and finally defeated the French in 1954. In that year an agreement was signed in Geneva, Switzerland, calling for the temporary division of Vietnam into two parts, one in the north and one in the south. The northern section kept the name Democratic Republic of Vietnam. Its government was led by communists, and in 1955 it adopted its present flag. The red is for revolution. The five points of the star stand for these five sections of the population: peasants, workers, intellectuals, young people, army.

The southern section kept the name Republic of Vietnam. Its leaders were anti-communist. In the ten years that followed, the government of South Vietnam was overthrown nine times, but each new government kept the flag of Bao Dai.

On December 20, 1963 appeared a new organization dedicated to overthrowing the government in South Vietnam. This revolutionary organization called itself the National Liberation Front of South Vietnam. It established an army known as the Vietcong, set up local governments in many areas, and adopted a flag similar to that of North Vietnam, except that it was half azure-blue and half red. The blue stands for peace.

The population of North Vietnam is 13,000,000 and there are 14,500,000 in South Vietnam. In both parts of the country the Viet people are the majority. There are more than forty minority groups, each with its own language or dialect. The language of the country as a whole is Vietnamese, and in the areas controlled by the Republic of Vietnam, Vietnamese is used in grade schools and high schools. French and English are used in colleges and universities. In National Liberation Front territory and in North Vietnam the Vietnamese language is used in colleges, as well as in lower schools. Buddhists are the largest religious group. There are other sects, including these: Hoa Hao, Cao-Daist, Binh-Xuyen, Catholic, Protestant.

WESTERN SAMOA (sah-MOH-uh): Polynesian explorers reached the volcanic islands of Western Samoa about 1000 B.C. The first Europeans visited there in 1722 and in 1830, a Christian missionary from England came to stay. After that, England, the United States and Germany all conducted business on the islands. Then, in 1900, the United States took control of Eastern Samoa, and Germany began to rule Western Samoa. New Zealand took Western Samoa away from Germany after World War I, and ruled it with the approval of the League of Nations. Following World War II, the Samoans sought independence. In 1948, the two kings who shared leadership agreed on a design for a flag. It has been used since January 1, 1962, when Western Samoa became the first fully independent Polynesian state. Samoans say the red in their flag stands for courage, the white for purity and the blue for freedom. The 130,000 citizens of Western Samoa speak Samoan, which is used, along with English, by the government and in the schools.

ZAMBIA (ZAM-bee-uh): British rule of Northern Rhodesia ended in 1964, and this African country became independent under the name of Zambia. The 3,600,000 Zambians belong to 79 tribes, each with its own language or dialect. Nearly half of the children under 15 are in schools, where the language they use is English. The flying eagle in the flag symbolizes freedom and the ability of the country to rise above its problems. Red represents the struggle for freedom. Black stands for the people of Zambia. Green represents the rich countryside. Orange stands for mineral wealth.

UNITED NATIONS: In April, 1945, preparations were being made for a conference in San Francisco that would establish the United Nations. Some of the people who did the planning thought it would be appropriate to have a symbol. The result was a map showing most of the world, with the North Pole at its centre. In December, 1946, the General Assembly of the United Nations approved a slightly revised design that depicted the *whole* world and indicated that the organization was meant to include every country. Two olive branches were added as a symbol of peace. The olive branch has stood for peace since the days of ancient Rome. On October 20, 1947, at its second session, the General Assembly adopted a flag that had this emblem on a blue ground.

Note: Barbados, in the West Indies, and Lesotho (previously Basutoland) in Africa, became independent states in 1966.

115

WHEN DID WARS BEGIN?

DURING most of the two million years that men have lived on earth, there were no great wars. Individuals sometimes fought. So did tribes. But the battles were not carefully planned on a big scale. The weapons were not very good. Fighting did not last very long. People did not have time for long drawn-out campaigns, because they had to spend most of their energy looking for food.

What we call war, fought by trained armies, began only after farmers could produce more food than they themselves needed. Rulers were then able to feed soldiers, and the king in one city could send his army out to seize wealth from another. Of course, each raid was likely to stir up an answering raid. These small but fierce wars were fought five thousand years ago in somewhat the same way that big ones between countries have been fought in recent times. The great difference has been that armies have had more and more inventions to use, and so wars have become more and more destructive. Finally, when atomic weapons appeared, people in many countries began trying to see how war could be abolished.

WHY DID THE HUNDRED YEARS' WAR LAST SO LONG?

MUCH of the time between 1337 and 1453, English and French rulers fought wars for the control of France. All these wars together are called the Hundred Years' War. It took that much time for the French to win. Both sides lost a great many men in battle, and they were weakened by other disasters, too. A terrible epidemic called the Black Death killed almost half the people. From time to time, soldiers looted and destroyed towns and farms. Greedy and cruel landlords and nobles robbed and killed peasants. Misery was so great that people tried several times to revolt. On top of everything else, fear spread because thousands of men and women were being tried for witchcraft and burned at the stake.

For these and other reasons, France did not start on the road to victory until 1429. That year an amazing thing happened. A peasant girl named Joan of Arc persuaded French leaders to give her command of an army against the British. At the head of ten thousand men, she won important battles. The exhausted country took courage and began to have a sense of national pride.

Before the war was over, Joan fell into the hands of the English. They soon arranged for her to be imprisoned and tried by the Church as a witch. In 1431, when she was only nineteen years old, Joan was found guilty and burned to death. Meantime, the war continued — but from then on, the French armies were the winners.

WHO INVENTED TAXES?

So FAR AS we know, taxes began in the cities of Sumer, which were ruled by kings about 5,500 years ago. At that time a king was often a combination of priest and ruler — almost a god. To this sacred person the common people brought gifts of food. In the beginning, he and his household and his assistants may have lived on whatever the people freely offered. Later, rulers told each farmer and fisherman and craftsman just how big his gift should be. In that way, taxes began.

Taxes offered a way of sharing the extra things that a man could produce but didn't absolutely need for himself. Sometimes a tax collector or a government used this surplus to provide services for the whole community, sometimes not. But from that day to this, governments have depended on taxes to keep their countries going.

Out of taxes grew writing. It happened this way: People brought more and more things to the ruler's sacred storehouse, which was part of the temple, and the temple priests had to account for everything. Otherwise, someone might get by without paying his tax. The early tax records were simply pictures of animals, baskets of grain and other tax-gifts. These little drawings were the first form of writing in Sumer. From them, modern writing developed.

The ancient Sumerian symbols do not look much like modern writing, but experts can read them. They were pressed into small chunks of wet clay, and when the clay tablets were baked, they turned into brick. Thousands of them have lasted from that day to this, buried in the ruins of old cities. As a result, we know a great deal about the oldest civilization, as well as the oldest taxes, in the world.

In the beginning, tax collectors simply took a share of whatever people produced. Later, when money was invented, the collectors accepted it in place of grain or fruit or fish. Money made it possible to have new taxes of many different kinds. At one time or another there have been taxes on such things as boats, divorces, windows, horse-race bets, and even the right to vote.

WHO WAS "THE LIBERATOR"?

IN 1783 a boy was born in a certain aristocratic family in Venezuela. As he grew up, he had his own private teachers. One of them taught him to read the work of Englishmen who had new-fangled ideas about democracy. He also read what had been written by men who made the French Revolution. Then, when he was travelling in Europe, he met a great German scientist, Alexander von Humboldt, who had been exploring in South America. Von Humboldt believed that Venezuela and other parts of South America would be better off if they were not ruled by Spain. Indeed, the German said, the Spanish colonies were ready to revolt.

The young Venezuelan next went to visit the United States where he met men who believed in democracy. Finally, with his head full of ideas he had gathered from great men in France, England, Germany and the United States, he returned to South America. There he set about organizing and leading people who wanted freedom. Before he died in 1830, he led armies that liberated from Spain the countries now called Colombia, Panama, Venezuela, Ecuador, Peru and Bolivia. This last country was named for the Liberator himself. His name was Simón Bolívar.

Santa Cruz Islanders in the South Pacific made red feathers into doughnut-shaped money.

WHO INVENTED MONEY?

IMAGINE that you are living in prehistoric times. You have caught more fish than your family can eat. Instead of letting them spoil, you decide to exchange them for something else that you may be able to use. A man in the next village has more baskets than he needs, and you go to see him. The basket-maker can use your fish, but he says they aren't worth as much as his baskets. He wants something more, or he won't trade. You offer him some beautiful sea shells, which he likes, and the deal is made.

The next time you go to the neighbouring village, the basket-maker has no baskets to give you in exchange for fish, so he offers you some of the sea shells, instead. You accept the sea shells, because you can trade them to still another man who has some rope that you want.

The shells are a form of money. They make trading easy because you and the other people have agreed on their value: a certain number of shells are worth this many fish, or that many baskets, or so much rope. Money can be anything you and the others choose. A shell, a woven mat, a big stone, a blanket, or pretty feathers are just as good as metal coins or paper bills. All of these things, and many others, have actually served as money. In some places, an animal skin has been used as the measure of value. One skin might buy a certain number of arrows, or a number of skins might buy a live sheep. In many places, cattle served as money.

120

Money has been used for so long a time that we can not tell who invented it or when. Babylonians may have been the first to make metal coins. Then, about 700 B.C., a people called the Lydians, who lived in what is now Turkey, began to put marks on coins to show how much they weighed. The weight indicated how much each coin was worth. Later, the Persians spread a uniform money system throughout their huge empire. It was a great help to Persian traders to have the same kind of money wherever they went.

Soon after A.D. 800, the Chinese started the use of paper money, which was easier to carry than gold or silver or copper coins. This idea has spread around the world. Each paper bill is like a letter from a ruler or a government saying, "We have plenty of valuable gold or silver in our storehouses. You can come and exchange this paper for it if you want to carry the heavy stuff away." As long as people believe that this is an honest statement, they need not bother with actual gold or silver.

American pioneers sometimes used animal skins as money. In those days, deer were plentiful, and hunters had quantities of buckskins which they sometimes called simply *bucks*. That is why some experts believe that an American may be using an old frontier expression when he says, "I have two bucks" for "I have two dollars."

STONE MONEY USED ON THE ISLAND OF YAP

NORTHWEST COAST INDIAN BLANKET USED AS MONEY

ANCIENT GREEK COIN

COPPER COIN USED IN CENTRAL AFRICA

WHEN DID TRADE UNIONS START?

ABOUT TWO HUNDRED years ago, a great many new machines and practical inventions came into being in Europe. Factories opened up, and coal was needed to run them, so mining increased. Thousands of men, women and children went to work in the growing industries, first in England and then in America.

The wages people earned in the factories were often very low, and the hours were very long. Adults worked sixteen hours a day, from six in the morning till ten at night, six days a week. Boys dug coal and tended furnaces in glass factories. Five-year-old girls tended machines in cloth factories. The children worked twelve or fourteen hours, six days a week.

Hoping to get better pay and shorter hours, people who worked in various trades joined together in organizations called unions. The members of these trade unions found that they could often succeed if they all stopped work until the employers agreed to give them what they wanted. This was called a strike. An employer could not make money while a strike was going on. On the other hand, workers could not eat unless they had wages. So they didn't always win, because hunger forced them to go back to work. But gradually, through strikes or threats of strikes, or just good bargaining, unions helped their members to get better wages. The working day grew shorter, until it was eight hours or seven hours instead of sixteen. At the

122

same time, many businesses that employed union members continued to make money, and some of them managed to become very big and rich.

The first modern union started in England in 1752. For a long time after that, unions were forbidden by law. But they continued, anyway. They simply avoided the word *union* and called themselves such things as "friendly societies." In 1824, some of the earlier English laws were repealed, and unions began to grow rapidly.

In the United States the shoemakers of Philadelphia formed a union in 1792, and in 1799 they went on strike. Some historians say there was a union even before that. Printers in New York belonged to it, and they conducted a strike in 1786.

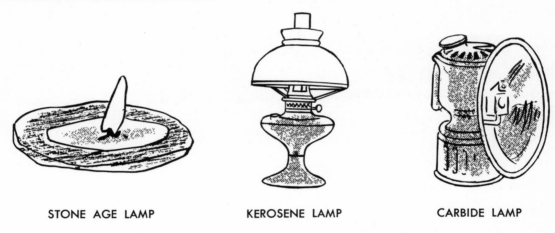

STONE AGE LAMP   KEROSENE LAMP   CARBIDE LAMP

WHEN WERE LIGHTS INVENTED?

STONE AGE people invented oil lamps at least fifteen thousand years ago. They were nothing but saucers filled with animal fat in which a string of some sort floated. When the oil-soaked string was lighted, it burned with a smoky flame.

From the Stone Age until the eighteenth century, nobody managed to invent a much better light. In the 1780's, a Swiss chemist found how to make an oil lamp that burned without smoking very much. In the next fifty years, lights got still better because better fuels were discovered. One fuel was made of turpentine and alcohol. Kerosene was another. And one inventor used a mixture of gasoline, sulphur, rusty nails and onions! Electric lamps came only about a century after the first good oil lamp.

WHO WERE THE FIRST CAPITALISTS?

EVERYBODY in ancient Sumer knew that if you planted one basketful of barley you could reap many basketfuls. If you owned cattle, there would be more when the cattle had calves. Wealth, in the form of grain or animals, would multiply. Then, when Sumerians began to use money, it seemed natural that this kind of wealth should also multiply. Men who had money let others use it for a while. In return, however, the lenders expected it to grow while the borrowers had it. A borrower was required to give back a larger sum than he had borrowed — in other words, he paid interest on the loan. Thus, men could get rich simply by lending and then collecting interest.

The money that a Sumerian lent was called *sag,* which was also the word for *head*. This word became attached to the moneylending idea, and when the idea spread to neighbouring lands, people translated *sag* into their own languages. Money for lending kept the name *head*. In Hebrew, the word was *rosh*. In Greek, *head* was *kefalaion*. In Latin, it was *caput*. In England, the word became *capital,* which comes from the Latin *caput*.

The Sumerians were the first capitalists, between 3000 and 2000 B.C., but Sumerian kings never let the moneylenders become very important. In Europe, capitalists only began to have real influence at the end of the Middle Ages. After that, their power grew steadily. They started banks for lending money, and they also used their capital to build factories which were the beginning of modern industry. (It is now customary to say that the factories themselves are also capital.)

Today, countries that do not believe in capitalism still use capital! Their governments, or their government banks, supply money to factories and farms.

WHO WERE THE FIRST COMMUNISTS?

IN 1843, when he was twenty-four years old, a man named Karl Marx was editor of a newspaper in the city of Cologne in the Kingdom of Prussia. Marx was in favor of democracy, and he also wrote some articles about socialism. Soon the Prussian police stopped the newspaper, and Marx went to Paris. There he wrote articles which the French police did not like. They made him leave the country. Finally he settled in England where he met another German, Friedrich Engels, who managed a factory that his father owned. The two young men decided that capitalism had flaws that could never be corrected and that the world needed a new system which they called communism.

In 1847, Marx and Engels gathered together a number of refugees from Germany, France, Italy, Russia and Switzerland and started the Communist League. To explain the ideas of this organization, they wrote a small book called *The Communist Manifesto,* which was published in 1848. Ever since then, the *Manifesto* has had tremendous influence. Perhaps no document, except the Bible, has been translated into more languages. By 1966, more than a third of the people in the world lived under governments headed by men who believed in communism. Although modern ideas of communism began in the middle of the nineteenth century, some of them came from earlier times. As with most of man's inventions, it isn't easy to say exactly when those ideas first began.

WHO REALLY DISCOVERED AMERICA?

In 1497 an Italian sea captain landed on the coast of North America. He had adopted an English name, John Cabot, and he sailed in an English vessel. Many people believed that this made Cabot and his English crew the real discoverers of North America.

In that same year, 1497, another Italian, Amerigo Vespucci, was on a vessel that touched the coast of South America. Of course, the Italian Christopher Columbus had already crossed the Atlantic Ocean in a Spanish ship, and had found islands in the Caribbean Sea. But he did not visit South America until after the voyage of Amerigo Vespucci. Columbus did not discover either North or South America.

These facts have been well-known for a long time. But a few scholars suspected there was more to the story than that. Was it possible that people called vikings, from Norway, crossed the Atlantic Ocean about five hundred years before Columbus did? Old Norse legends said so. They told of a voyage made by Leif Ericson to a place he called Vinland, west of Greenland, but no one had proof that the tales were true. Then, in 1961, an archeologist dug up the remains of a settlement in Newfoundland. Tools

126

and other objects proved that this was not an Indian village. Vikings had been there, possibly about A.D. 1000.

Finally, in 1965, Yale University announced that it had a map showing where Vinland was. The map had been drawn fifty-two years before the voyage of Columbus. It showed Vinland along the northeast coast of North America, and it said definitely that this place was discovered by Leif Ericson. The old legends were right. Leif apparently did land in the New World about A.D. 1000. The map showed that he thought Vinland was only a big island. He did not know he had discovered a continent.

Was the map genuine? Or could it be a fake? Experts studied it with great care. At last, they said it had indeed been made about the year 1440. The rest of the story is still a bit of a mystery. Someone in Basel, Switzerland, seems to have copied the map from an older one. But why in 1440? Probably the explanation is this: About that time Christian churchmen from many countries were meeting in Basel to exchange information. One man described a journey that a European monk had made to Mongolia in the thirteenth century. A man from Scandinavia also had a marvelous story to tell — the tale of Leif's voyage to a new land. As proof, the churchman must have brought with him an old map, from which a copy was made. This copy, together with the handwritten story of the journey to Mongolia, was then bound into a book. And everybody forgot about it. The map came to light again only a few years ago when an American bought the book and gave it to Yale University.

Even though the vikings reached the New World before Columbus, they were not the first people in America. The Indians came ahead of them — at least twelve thousand years ago. And about five thousand years ago a boat from Japan landed on the coast of Ecuador. There is no book or map about the Japanese voyage. But scientists have some very convincing evidence that it happened. They have found ancient pottery buried deep in the earth in Ecuador, and it is the kind of pottery made by the Japanese five thousand years ago.

So the fact is that no one person or nation can claim the great discovery. It took many people from many nations to put the New World into our maps. That's the way it often is with discoveries.

WHO WAS THE FIRST MAN TO GO AROUND THE WORLD?

ON MONDAY, September 7, 1522, a little vessel called the *Vittoria* entered the port of Seville in Spain. The *Vittoria* needed repairs, and the thirteen men on board had difficulty handling her. Indeed, they had difficulty handling themselves. They were all weak from hunger and disease.

The first thing the tattered little band of sailors did when they got ashore was to walk barefoot, carrying lighted candles, to a nearby shrine. There they offered thanks for their return to Spain. They also asked forgiveness for having celebrated Mass on Monday instead of on Sunday, the holy day that Catholics had set aside for religious worship.

There was a reason why these sailors had got so mixed up that they mistook Monday for Sunday: They had sailed completely around the earth, and they had lost a day, just as travellers still do when they circle the globe! But the *Vittoria* was the first ship ever to make the voyage, and no one could understand the strange trick their calendar seemed to have played on them.

The thirteen men on the *Vittoria* were all who remained alive out of 265 who had set sail three years before under the command of Fernando de Magalhaes, usually called Ferdinand Magellan. He himself had been killed by Filipinos when he told them they must either become Christians or be slaughtered.

Because the *Vittoria* was one of the five vessels that had started out under Magellan's command, some people have believed that Magellan himself sailed around the world. Actually, the commander of the ship that did complete this important voyage was Juan Sebastian del Cano. He and the other twelve men on the *Vittoria* deserve the credit. Magellan had never even planned to go around the world!

128

WHEN WAS THE NORTH POLE DISCOVERED?

IN 1909, a party of six men reached for the first time the point on the ice-covered Arctic Ocean that is called the North Pole. One was white, one a Negro and four were Eskimos. The white man, Admiral Robert E. Peary, and the Negro, Matthew A. Henson, came from the United States.

WHEN WAS THE SOUTH POLE DISCOVERED?

ON THE CONTINENT of Antarctica, toward the end of 1911, two teams of explorers started a race for the South Pole. One team was Norwegian. Its leader, Roald Amundsen, and his four companions had Eskimo dogs that pulled sleds loaded with their supplies. The other team of five men was led by an English naval captain, Robert F. Scott. The Englishmen had both a motor-driven tractor and sleds pulled by sturdy Siberian ponies. Very soon the tractor broke down. Then the ponies began to die. Before long, there were none left, and the men had to pull their heavy sleds.

Both teams struggled up onto the high Antarctic plateau in intense cold. In spite of their special difficulties, the Englishmen kept on and finally reached the South Pole, which is 9,500 feet above sea level. There they found a tent, already pitched. Over it flew the flag of Norway, and inside was a letter from Amundsen who had arrived there on December 14.

The five brave Englishmen, already exhausted, could not make it back to their starting point. They died along the way, but the record that Robert Scott kept was later found, along with the film of a photograph showing him and the Norwegian tent and flag he found at the South Pole.

129

MAKING PARCHMENT

WHAT WERE ANCIENT BOOKS LIKE?

THE FIRST BOOKS were stories and poems, histories, prayers, law records. Writers made them by scratching words on cakes of moist clay. When the clay was baked, it formed hard tablets that lasted a long time. Whole libraries of these five-thousand-year-old tablets have been found in Mesopotamia.

Egyptians made books of two kinds. Record books, which people used and handled over and over, were written on leather. For ordinary reading a more fragile material did well enough. It was a kind of paper made from a plant called the papyrus reed. Using brushes and ink, men painted words on long strips of papyrus. Then the strips were rolled up and stored in containers. Greeks and Romans also had books hand-written on rolls of papyrus obtained from Egypt. When they could not get it, they used a material called parchment.

The first parchment was not intended for books. Men in Asia used it for their drums perhaps three thousand years ago. They made it from goat-skin or calfskin which they soaked and then scraped with a special knife until it was very thin. The finished parchment was white and so strong and tough that the Romans began using it for permanent record scrolls.

In the Middle Ages, Christian monks made books on parchment, but not in the form of scrolls. Instead, they cut each skin up into four or five sheets which they sewed together at the left edge. Then with pen and colored inks they copied such things as the Bible, prayer books, or accounts of travels and natural wonders. The copying took a long time. The parchment itself was expensive, so it is no wonder that the King of England in 1331 had to pay as much for one book as he did for ninety oxen.

130

Sometimes one monk would read aloud from a book to a whole group of others who were called scribes. The scribes copied down what he dictated, and in this way several new books could be made at one time. Scholars who can read old handwriting occasionally find small errors in some of the copying. (Perhaps the scribe did not hear correctly, or perhaps he was just daydreaming.)

The Maya Indians wrote their books on paper made of bark that they pulled in long strips from wild fig trees. After the bark had been soaked and washed, it was beaten with paddles to stretch it out thin and wide. A finished book, written by hand, was about fifteen feet long. Instead of rolling the paper up, as the Egyptians did, the Mayas folded it back and forth, accordion fashion. Other Central American Indians had this same kind of book.

Early Chinese books were handwritten in a kind of varnish on slabs of wood or strips of bamboo. Later, perhaps about A.D. 100, a Chinese inventor made paper from bark and rags. Books were soon being written on paper — a thousand years before the idea finally reached Europe.

An English scribe in the Middle Ages copied only the words in a book. Then an artist copied the illustrations. This is part of a page in *The Bestiary*, a book about animals.

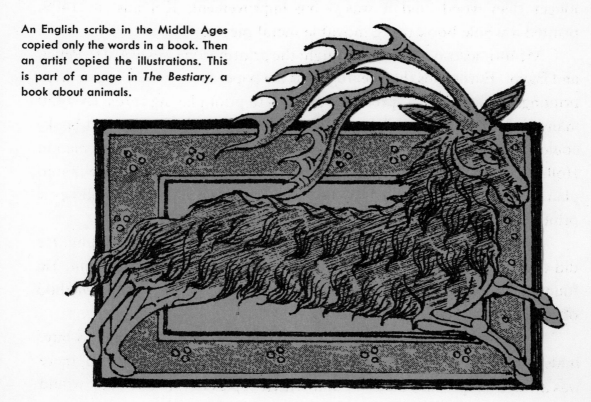

WHO INVENTED PRINTING?

ONCE THERE was a certain Chinese boy who loved to read, but he had to borrow books from his friends because he was very poor. In those days — a little over a thousand years ago — all books were written by hand, and so they cost a great deal. The boy's friends did not really like to lend anything so valuable. This shamed him. Still, he kept reading, and he decided to do something about books when he grew up. He did. He invented printing.

To make the first books, a craftsman carved the words for a whole page into a single block of wood. The block was then used to print the page. Later, the Chinese began to use a separate small piece of wood for each word. These could be fitted into slots in a big block. The separate words could be used again and again, because the printer could move them around and put them into any kind of combination with other word-pieces. Then someone invented movable type made from metal. Metal lasted longer than wood, and it was a big improvement. Koreans, in 1409, printed a whole book using movable metal pieces.

Meantime, travellers had brought the printing idea westward to Persia and Egypt. Europeans then heard about the paper money the Chinese were printing. In Germany, a special shop began to print playing cards. By 1450 many craftsmen in various countries were familiar with the idea that books could be printed from metal type. Frenchmen tried it. At least one man in Holland did. A German, Johann Gutenberg, seems to have been the first to plan a really big project. In 1454 he started to produce the first Bibles ever printed from movable type.

Gutenberg is sometimes given credit for the invention of printing. He did not invent it, but he did something else that was very important. He found a combination of metals that would make good type and a method of shaping the letters conveniently.

Printing soon made books cheap enough for ordinary people to buy. It also made the world safer for books. Before printing was invented, there was always danger that the few handwritten copies of any one book would

be destroyed. For example, the greatest library of the ancient world — more than half a million books — was burned in A.D. 270, when the city of Alexandria in Egypt was invaded. Another huge collection of books was lost during the Middle Ages in raids on Constantinople. Almost all of the works of several great writers completely disappeared.

In China a tyrannical emperor once burned all books except those dealing with medicine or farming. Now, he thought, it would be impossible for anyone to say that rulers in the past had been better than he. When four hundred stubborn men refused to give up their books, he had them all executed. This happened in 212 B.C., but historians now can't be sure about things that happened in China before that date. During the Middle Ages, European church officials often burned books they didn't like. In the sixteenth century a Spanish bishop ordered the destruction of all books that had been hand-written in the Maya Indian language. Only a few of these are known to have been saved.

Even after printing began, men sometimes tried to destroy books. When an Englishman, William Tyndale, argued that all people should be able to read the Bible, church officials disagreed with him. They burned six thousand copies of the New Testament which Tyndale had translated into English in 1526. In 1933, German Nazis encouraged students at Berlin University to burn 25,000 books by "un-German" writers, and school children in other cities made similar bonfires. But thanks to printing, there were other copies of these books in existence. One destructive act could not remove them entirely from the world.

133

HOW DID SLAVERY BEGIN?

MOST SLAVES in ancient times were prisoners of war. Their conquerors made them work in gangs, doing heavy labour on big farms. Raiders sometimes attacked cities simply to capture slaves, and they seized men, women and children from wandering tribes. Gang slaves were put to work building canals and digging in mines. Chained to benches, they pulled the huge oars of seagoing ships.

As trade grew, craftsmen were able to sell more goods than they could produce. They needed help, and they often bought slaves and trained them. But not all slaves were prisoners of war. Many a free man borrowed money, then could not pay it back, and sold himself to the moneylender. Or he sold his wife or children. In one tribe a medicine man could be sold if his cures did not work.

Twenty-five hundred years ago, some Greek cities regularly sent out pirate expeditions and armies of raiders to bring back not only loot but also captives who had special skills. These prisoners were turned into slaves in the city workshops. Along with free craftsmen, they produced quantities of beautiful things that traders sold.

On the coast of Arabia there are still slaves who serve as teachers.

Many Greeks grew wealthy, and so they had leisure to study and think. They learned a great deal about mathematics. They discovered how the power of steam could be harnessed, and they could have gone on to invent all kinds of useful machines if they had wanted to. But they didn't. Machines interested them only as curiosities or toys. In fact, the learned men discouraged practical inventions. Thanks to slavery, they had every comfort they wanted, and they scorned anyone who bothered his head with ordinary everyday affairs. All craftsmen, both free men and slaves, were looked down upon, and there was little reason to make new inventions. After a while, no one even remembered the discoveries that might have brought modern science to the world many years sooner.

At one time or another, members of every race and almost every nationality have been slaves and slave-owners. White people from Britain were slaves in ancient Rome. Chinese have been both owners and slaves. So have Africans. Europeans who invaded America did not find it easy to keep Indian slaves. They brought people from Africa, instead. This was not because any one race is better suited to slavery than another. It just happened that Africans could not run away and get back home to friends and relatives. Indians could — and did.

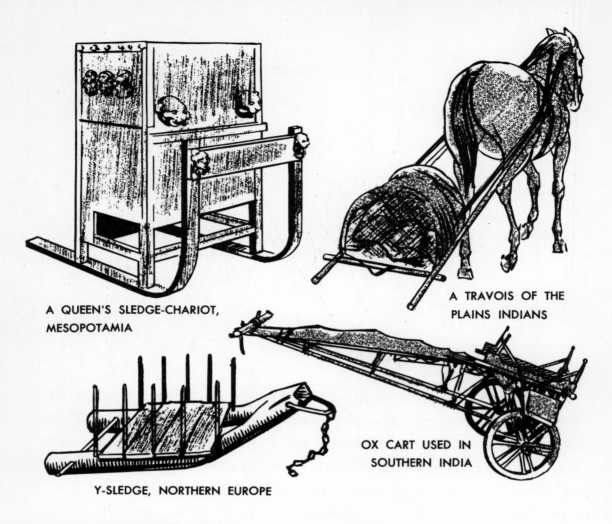

A QUEEN'S SLEDGE-CHARIOT, MESOPOTAMIA

A TRAVOIS OF THE PLAINS INDIANS

Y-SLEDGE, NORTHERN EUROPE

OX CART USED IN SOUTHERN INDIA

WHO INVENTED THE AUTOMOBILE?

WHEELS had to be invented before there could be automobiles, and wheels first appeared in ancient Mesopotamia about five thousand years ago. Before that, loads were often carried on sleds — and not just in places where snow fell. A sled's runners would slide fairly well over sand, pine needles, grass or even mud. (Some people think that milk may have been poured on the ground to make it very slippery for very heavy loads.)

Before wheels were invented, a man might also tie a burden onto two poles that made a V-shape when they were attached to a harness on a pack animal. Later, when he put these poles up on wheels, he had a cart. Two carts joined together made a four-wheeled wagon. So did a sled with four wheels attached.

For a very long time the power that moved wagons came from the muscles of animals or men. In 1705 an Englishman named Thomas Newcomen patented the first practical steam engine, but its power was used only for such things as pumping water. Muscle power still turned the wheels that moved loads until 1763, when a Frenchman, Nicolas Joseph Cugnot, attached a steam engine to a wagon. That was the first automobile.

The steam that drove Cugnot's wheels came from a boiler heated by a fire outside the engine itself. Almost a hundred years later, in 1859, another Frenchman found a way of using energy from ordinary cooking-stove gas that burned inside an engine. Soon the *internal combustion* engine was driving a wagon. This was not actually the first such engine. Long before, in 1680, a Dutchman named Christian Huyghens had built one that used gunpowder, not gas. But Huyghens did not see a practical use for his invention.

Two Germans made improvements in the gas-burning engine. Other men found a way to use oil instead of stove gas in an automobile engine. Gottlieb Daimler then built engines that could use gasoline. The first gasoline automobile in America was built by two brothers, Charles and Frank Duryea, in 1892.

It took all of these inventions — plus a great many others from many countries — to develop the modern automobile. No one person and no one country can claim all the credit. For a special reason, England made almost no automobile inventions at first. Until 1896, there was an English law that discouraged the use of automobiles. It required a man carrying a red flag to walk ahead of any vehicle that was driven by a motor!

The first automobile — a steam engine on a wagon!

WHO MADE THE FIRST CALENDAR?

NIGHT always follows day, and day follows night. Over and over again, a sliver of moon appears in the night sky; then, in the nights that follow, it rounds out, slims down again, and disappears. Year after year the leaves bud on trees, grow big, then fall to the ground. These events and many others repeat and repeat and repeat. Of course, early men noticed them. They noticed, too, that certain combinations of stars appeared again and again. Some combinations could be seen when the seasons were changing on earth. To keep track of these heavenly and earthly events, certain Stone Age men apparently made marks on rocks, reindeer bones and mammoth tusks. Recently, archeologists have found some of these marked objects, which may be man's first efforts to make a calendar.

STONEHENGE

Other men set up tall blocks of stone to make a kind of calendar. Some of these huge pillars are still standing at Stonehenge in England. There, at least 3,300 years ago, men studied the sky. By watching where the sun's rays lighted up certain places among the pillars, they could tell what time of the year it was.

Ancient sky-watchers also measured time by the moon. The days between two full moons made a month. (The English word *month* is related to the word *moon*.)

Weeks came into the calendar, not from a study of the sky, but from the habits of men. A week was simply the time between market days.

People who wanted to trade with each other found it convenient to meet at regular times, and when they met, they enjoyed themselves. Some gathered every tenth day, some every eighth day, others every third or fourth day.

The Babylonians traded and relaxed every seventh day. This custom spread to many places around the Mediterranean Sea. The Romans adopted it and passed it along to western Europe and Britain. Some of the people who were conquered by the Romans accepted Roman names for the seven days in their week. Others gave the days names of their own. In Britain there was a compromise. Sunday, sacred to the sun, and Monday, sacred to the moon, are Roman ideas with English names. The next four days were named for ancient gods of the Saxon tribes who drove the Romans out of Britain: Tuesday for Tiw, god of war; Wednesday for Woden, leader of the gods; Thursday for Thor, the thunder god; and Friday for Frigge, Woden's wife. Saturday goes back to Saturn, the Roman god of the crops and harvest.

The names of the months, in English, are based on old Roman names. July was to commemorate Julius Caesar, who took an interest in improving the inaccurate calendar which Romans had borrowed from Egypt. The trouble lay in the odd length of the year — that is, the length of time it takes for the earth to go around the sun. The year does not consist of an exact number of whole days. Instead, it is 365 days long, plus 6 hours, 48 minutes and 46 seconds. The Egyptian calendar had 365 days, but did not allow for this partial extra day. As a result, the calendar began to lag behind the actual date. In 46 B.C., Caesar ordered changes that helped to make it more dependable.

Caesar's calendar still wasn't perfect. After a while it, too, got out of gear with the seasons. In the sixteenth century it was changed by Pope Gregory XIII, who was a powerful ruler as well as head of the Roman Catholic Church. On the advice of the best astronomers, he added leap years to the calendar, and we still have them today.

The word *calendar* itself comes from the name of the day on which the Romans thought that all bills should be paid.

SHIVA IS ONE OF THE
MANY HINDU GODS

WHEN DID THE HINDU RELIGION BEGIN?

HINDUISM began in prehistoric times, and no one can tell exactly when. It grew up gradually and changed as different kinds of people moved into India. The first to live there seem to have been small people called Negritos. Next came people who were much like the natives of Australia. Later, there were immigrants from far to the west, possibly from Asia Minor or even from Europe. Each new incoming wave brought people who had their own religious ideas.

All of these different ideas seemed to stay alive in India, and they became part of one complicated religion. New beliefs were not excluded. It is the spirit of Hinduism to "live and let live," said Jawaharlal Nehru, the leader of India who died in 1964. Today, two-thirds of the 450 million people who live in India are Hindus.

The word Hindu is not nearly so old as the religion itself. In fact, it was not used until Moslems began to invade India in A.D. 1001.

WHEN DID THE BUDDHIST RELIGION BEGIN?

MORE THAN five hundred years before the birth of Christ, the Buddhist religion began to develop from the Hindu religion in India. There are now about 160,000,000 Buddhists in the world. Most of them live in Burma, Thailand, Ceylon, Japan and China. A small but growing number of people in America and Europe are Buddhists. U Thant, a Buddhist from Burma, became Secretary-General of the United Nations in 1964.

140

WHEN DID MOHAMMEDANISM START?

IN THE YEAR 610 an Arab named Mohammed began building a new religion which later developed its own calendar. The official date upon which this calendar starts is July 16, 622, according to the Christian calendar. That was the day when followers of Mohammed entered the town of Medina in Arabia and pursuaded many of its inhabitants to join them.

The followers of Mohammed do not call themselves Mohammedans. They say they are Moslems, or Muslims, and they call their religion Islam. In many ways, Islam grew out of the Jewish and Christian religions, although Moslems read a book called the Koran rather than the Bible. Islam is now divided into several sects or denominations. The largest of these is the Sunnite. Another is the Shi-ite. About one-seventh of the people in the world are Moslems.

From very ancient times Shinto has been a religion in Japan. Today there are more than 100,000 shrines where Shinto ceremonies are held.

In the sixth century B.C. the Chinese people were made miserable by constant wars between powerful ambitious noblemen. At this time a young man named Kung began to teach his belief in a great society in which rulers and people were peaceful, wise, just and loving. His teachings spread and became a kind of religion without gods. People called him Kung fu-tze, which was something like saying "Kung, the professor." Today, there are still many followers of Confucianism in Asia.

141

WHAT WERE THE FIRST CLOTHES LIKE?

WE HAVE to guess about this because all the very oldest clothes have apparently rotted away. We do know what people wear in parts of the world that have been touched very little by modern civilization. In some places they wear only paint or tattooed designs which may cover most of the body. Some wear just a bracelet or a bit of string. Others make skirts and aprons of grass, of big leaves cut in strips, of pounded tree bark, of feathers woven together with cord. In very cold places they wear suits of fur.

The Indians who lived at the tip of South America did not dress warmly, in spite of the cold. They went about barefoot in the snow. They wrapped animal skins around their bare shoulders only in the iciest weather. This may mean that ancient men in cold climates did not bother much with clothes. Perhaps one such man flung a skin over his back at first just to boast that he was a good hunter. When he found it was pleasantly warm, he wore it for protection, too.

After women learned to sew, they made clothes like these.

One scientist believes that suits made of leather were invented at a time when a change in climate made game animals very scarce. Hunters got so hungry that they chewed even the skins of animals. Chewing makes skins soft and easy to work with, and this may have started the kind of leather clothes that Stone Age tribes in northern Europe and Asia wore. Some of these leather clothes have been found in bogs where chemicals in the water helped to preserve them.

The oldest known cloth was woven about 8,500 years ago. It comes from a place in Turkey called Catal Huyuk. Of course, clothes of linen, wool or cotton may have been made before that, but if they were, they haven't lasted — or haven't been found. At any rate, people did not have much cloth in that part of the world until after plows were invented. This is why: Before there were plows, women hoed the fields, besides taking care of children and doing tasks around the house. This meant they were too busy for much weaving. But then, someone thought of harnessing an ox to a hoe. That was the first kind of plow, and field work became men's work, because men always took care of the animals. Women now had more time at home — time to weave and make clothes.

People in the old days wore clothes for protection against cold, and also to keep off the hot sun — and for still another reason. They covered parts of the body that they felt should be covered for the sake of modesty. Different people have different ideas about this, but they usually believe that some part of the body should not be seen. Of course, this had an effect on clothing. In New Guinea, a girl felt ashamed if she did not have an earring in her ear, although she wore very little else. At the same time, these dark-skinned people of New Guinea thought that Europeans who visited them probably wore so many clothes because they were ashamed of their white skins.

That misunderstanding did no harm. But the same kind of mistake killed off many Indians on the northwest coast of America. There the white missionaries persuaded the Indians that it was not proper to undress when they came inside the big houses where many families lived together. The Indians began sitting around in damp clothes — the weather is very rainy there — and a great many of them soon died of pneumonia.

WHO INVENTED TROUSERS?

Tribes that lived in northern parts of Europe and Asia invented trousers. Then people who lived farther south borrowed the idea. Because the Roman rulers feared these northern tribesmen and their growing influence, a law was made against trousers. In fact, any Roman could be executed for wearing them. During the Middle Ages the old Roman prejudice died out.

In Asia, both men and women adopted trousers, and the custom continues to this day in many places. In parts of Soviet Central Asia, girls still wear the old-fashioned ankle-length pantaloons — and over them a modern European kind of skirt.

MODERN NURSES IN PAKISTAN

WHY DID PEOPLE BEGIN TO WEAR JEWELRY?

PERHAPS JEWELRY was worn first because men thought or hoped there might be some magic in it. A bead made of amber would pick up bits of dry leaves if it was rubbed against fur or hair. That seemed magical. Perhaps necklaces of tiger teeth would give a man the cunning of a big cat. Grizzly bear claws might make him very strong.

At the same time, both men and women probably liked ornaments and decorations just for beauty. Women used lipstick and eyebrow pencil to improve their looks at least four thousand years ago. Instead of hair spray, which had not yet been invented, women in ancient Rome sometimes used a clay paste. Some African women still do. Almost all peoples on earth have tattooed decorations on their skins at some time in their history. Many groups have flattened their heads, lengthened necks, stretched ears or lips. They haven't always agreed on what makes a person beautiful or what brings luck. But they have always been sure that by tinkering and making an effort of some sort they could improve themselves or the world — or both.

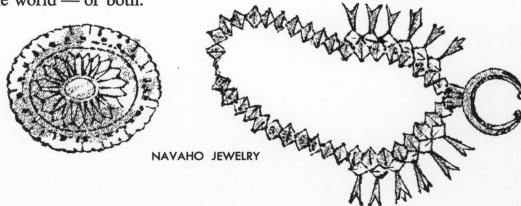

NAVAHO JEWELRY

WHY DON'T ALL PEOPLE DRESS ALIKE?

CLOTHES are a kind of language. They say, "I am a boy," or "I am a girl," or "I am a footballer," "I am a nurse," "I belong to a certain group." By wearing a white dress, a European or American bride tells us she hasn't been married before.

Protestant girls in Holland once wore round knobs on their head-dresses. Girls who wore square ones were Catholic. Moslem men wore green turbans to show they had been to the holy city of Mecca.

Almost everywhere in the world, women like to show by their dress that they are women, and men that they are men. Even where clothing is only the tiniest kind of apron, the woman's apron is usually different from the man's. This has been true since ancient times, as we know from paintings, carvings and pictures on pottery.

Until quite recently, almost all clothes also said in very plain language, "I am a noble," or "I belong to one of the lower classes." To be sure of this visible class distinction, rulers often made laws about dress and punished anyone who broke them. For example, in Japan there were strict rules about the clothes to be worn by each social group — and also about how each group spoke, walked, sat and prayed. The lower classes in ancient Peru were not allowed to wear ornaments of gold or silver. In France, at one time, when pointed shoes were popular, the law stated that common people could have sharp tips half a foot long; businessmen, one foot long; and the nobles, two feet long. Noble Frenchwomen could carry muffs of expensive fur, but all others had to settle for dog and cat fur. These laws were abolished at the time of the French Revolution.

There are still differences. Clothes vary from country to country. Within countries, classes do not always dress alike, but more and more fashions are becoming world-wide.

WHEN DID DANCING BEGIN?

EVER SINCE their first days on earth, people have been sociable. They love to be part of a group. This group feeling is so strong that it sometimes works even when you aren't thinking about it. At a baseball game, for example, your leg muscles sometimes tighten up when a player on your team starts to run. This same kind of unplanned moving-together may have led to the first dancing.

Men found that rhythm in motion was pleasant, and they invented many rhythms, then countless variations. Some danced fast and with their whole bodies, leaping and twisting. Some took only small, slow steps. In Indonesia, arms and hands are more active than feet. Polynesians dance sitting down. They simply keep time with the upper part of the body.

Human beings have usually included animals in their sociable feelings. (That may explain why we keep pets.) Early men may have admired an animal's power and hoped to capture its strength and speed by imitating it. So they wore animal costumes and copied animal motions in dances at ceremonies. Cave paintings in France that are at least 15,000 years old

JAPANESE DANCER   HAWAIIAN DANCER   INDIAN DANCER

show masked animal dancers, and bone pipes and whistles found in the caves indicate that music probably accompanied the dancing.

HOW DID APRIL FOOLS' DAY START?

FOR MANY HUNDREDS of years the Hindus in India have held a gay spring festival called Hoolee. It is always part of the fun during the holiday to send an unsuspecting person off on a foolish errand. Perhaps this idea spread from India to Europe and then to the United States. At any rate, many countries have a day of practical jokes which comes at the beginning or the end of April. It is often called All Fools' Day.

There is a story that in France, during the reign of King Louis XIII, a servant in a castle told a guard on April 1 that a prisoner was escaping. The guard thought that this was merely an April Fool joke and paid no attention. The result was that the prisoner did escape.

Mexico has a day — December 28 — on which people play practical jokes. If you are so foolish as to lend something on that day, the borrower doesn't have to give it back!

ANCIENT EGYPTIAN DANCER   BALINESE DANCER   CLOG DANCER (U.S.)

WHY IS NEW YEAR'S DAY A HOLIDAY?

EVER SINCE prehistoric times, people everywhere in the world have celebrated the beginning of a new year. Very often these celebrations in the northern part of the world came at midwinter — the time when days were beginning to get longer, after they had been very short.

In ancient Rome, Caesar's calendar fixed the beginning of the year on January 1. People cleaned and decorated their houses beforehand and gave children presents on that day. Americans and many others use a calendar based on Caesar's, and their New Year begins January 1.

The Jewish New Year is celebrated in the autumn, perhaps because at that time of year rains began to fall in Palestine and a new farming season could begin. The celebration lasts ten days. The first day is called Rosh Hashonah, which means *beginning of the year*. Part of the ceremony on that day is the blowing of a ram's horn. The sound of the horn is supposed to awaken people who have been sleeping and not doing their full duty. The ten-day period ends with Yom Kippur. This is the day that God is said to close the Book of Life for one year and to open a new Book of Life in which to keep a record of the next year. Religious Jews like to follow this example. They pay their debts before the end of the old year so they can start the new year without owing anybody anything.

The Moslem New Year festival is called Muharram. Its date on the Western calendar keeps changing because Moslems use a calendar based on phases of the moon, and so it has only 364 days instead of 365.

Muharram lasts for ten days, just as the Jewish New Year celebration does. In many places the first day of Muharram is very solemn. Men don't shave or wash and they wear the same kind of mourning clothes that are worn when someone dies. Toward evening they all go into the streets, and as they meet they wish each other a happy New Year. At the same time, they exchange coins. When a man gives a coin before he manages to utter his wish for a happy New Year, the man who receives the coin keeps it for the next twelve months to bring good luck.

The traditional Chinese New Year begins on the first day of the First Moon, according to the old Chinese calendar. This usually corresponds

Chinese who live in the United States celebrate the beginning of their New Year, but the festivities last only one day.

with a date early in February on the Western calendar. Preparations go on for a month before the festivities, which last for fifteen days. Houses are thoroughly cleaned. New red paint is put on the doors to keep evil spirits away. People all try to buy new clothes. At the very least, they get new shoes, for it would be bad luck to start the New Year in old ones.

On New Year's Eve, every family has a banquet at home. Nobody goes out. The next morning, people pour into the streets, and everyone pays his debts. From now on, for two weeks, players and musicians go through the streets giving entertainments. Then comes the final celebration — the Feast of the Lanterns. At night, crowds carrying lanterns join in a parade. At the head of the parade a long dragon made of paper or silk is carried by many men. It wriggles and winds about, but is not meant to be frightening. It is a symbol for good luck, and when it appears, people along the way set off firecrackers for fun.

HOW DID HOLIDAYS BEGIN?

THE WORD *holiday* comes from *holy day,* and that's just what it was in the beginning. All holidays had a connection with religion. Many of the most important holidays are still holy days.

On the island of Puerto Rico every town has a festival at some time during the year honouring its own special saint. In addition, all of the people celebrate the Feast of the Three Kings on January 6, twelve days after Christmas. The holiday is held in honour of the Three Wise Men who, the Bible story says, brought gifts to the child Jesus. Before the festival, Puerto Rican children write letters asking the Three Kings to bring them presents. On the eve of January 6, each child puts some grass under his bed, "to feed the Kings' camels," he says. The next morning he finds the grass gone and presents in its place. All day, boys dressed as the Kings go from house to house, singing songs and begging for pennies.

Mexico also celebrates the Feast of the Holy Kings on January 6, but there the children don't put grass in a box. Instead, they set their shoes out on balconies, just as boys and girls in other places hang up stockings on Christmas Eve. Mexicans hold festivals in honour of many Roman Catholic saints. They celebrate many ancient Indian festivals — and they have modern political holidays, too. The big national holiday comes on September 16. That was the day, in 1810, when Mexico's independence from Spain was declared by Miguel Hidalgo a priest and revolutionary leader. At night, crowds now gather in a great square called the Zócalo in Mexico City. The President comes out on the balcony of the National Palace which overlooks one end of the square. Then, at exactly eleven o'clock, the President shouts out the Mexican cry of independence: "Mexicans, long live our heroes! Long live our independence! Long live Mexico!" With that he rings a famous old bell. All the bells in the city start ringing, and there is a great outburst of high spirits from the people.

Mexicans have another holiday on March 21. That is the birthday of Benito Juarez, who was a famous president of Mexico. Juarez lived at the same time as Abraham Lincoln, and people honour him in the

same way that Lincoln is honoured in the United States. Because Juarez was an Indian, March 21 is called the Day of the Indian Child.

Some festivals seem to have no connection with religion, but really did start as days that were holy among pagan people. Take May Day, for example. In some districts, girls often dance around a tall pole on the first day of May, and one is chosen May Queen. This custom began ages ago when people danced around a sacred pole to celebrate the coming of new life in spring.

Another kind of May Day celebration began in the United States. On May 1, 1886, many working men in Chicago went on strike. Most of them had been working twelve hours a day, and they thought eight hours was enough. For many years afterward, working men in the United States gathered on the first of May to hold parades and hear speeches. Then the custom spread to other countries. Huge May Day parades are now held in Moscow, Peking and other cities under communist rule.

Batter made of corn meal is poured into a heated pit and baked to make a cake for a Navaho girl's growing-up ceremony.

WHY DO WE CELEBRATE BIRTHDAYS?

A BIRTHDAY CELEBRATION is one of man's very old customs. The idea must have started soon after people began to keep exact records of years and days. But the reason for the celebration is even older than that. It probably began when prehistoric mothers and fathers noticed that children seemed to grow up by stages. One day a baby could not walk, but the next day he took his first step. One day he gurgled; the next, he said a word. There were many such changes, and most of them must have seemed mysterious. Very often anything mysterious frightens human beings. They fear what is new and different. And so, long ago, changes came to mean danger. But people did not let fear stop them. It was part of being human to *do* something, take some action, try to ward off danger.

How could parents make sure their child would enter a new stage safely? One answer was to hold a ceremony. The right kind of ceremony might scare away evil spirits. Gifts to kindly spirits might bring protection. Gifts to the child encouraged him, and games played at the ceremony showed that he was growing skillful and strong. Today, at birthday parties,

154

the extra-big puff of breath that blows out all the candles is really a test of strength. It is a modern way of carrying on an old custom.

To many people, certain times of change seemed particularly risky. For example, when a boy was old enough to become a warrior, he would begin a new kind of life. Special ceremonies were held for him and often served to test his courage. In Guyana (formerly Guiana), Indian boys had to keep absolutely still when big poisonous ants bit them. In ancient Sparta, they had to bear pain without making a sound.

Today, newcomers in some schools are victims of practical jokes. This is a survival from the days when boys had to pass tests for bravery before they were considered men. Clubs, too, sometimes have initiations that resemble the ancient ceremonies for warding off evil spirits at a time of change. These customs may seem to have little to do with the modern world, but they are understandable if you remember that they go back to a time when men were trying to invent ways of solving the big mysterious problems of life.

In one part of Mexico, the birthday child wears a crown made from flowers and ears of corn.

INDEX

ACKNOWLEDGMENTS

For help in making this book possible, the authors want to thank N. O. Abelson, Map Librarian, United Nations; Prof. Dorothy Cross, Hunter College; Prof. Robert Ehrich, Brooklyn College; Nancy L. Gilbert, Assistant Librarian, American Automobile Association; Prof. Glenn Gray, University of Nebraska; C. K. Jones, Odhams Books, Ltd., London; Edwin M. Moser, Fairleigh Dickinson University; Robert Riley, Brooklyn Museum; Janet Siskind, Brooklyn College; the Permanent Missions of the new countries belonging to the United Nations; information officers of several countries not in the United Nations; and UNESCO, for the use of its photographic files.